THE MATTHEWS-NORTHRUP WORKS
BUFFALO N.Y.

DAR POINT'S MANY ATTRACTIONS, AS SEEN THROUGH THE CAMERA

shady and sequestered scene,
with laurels ever green, and
that for endless summer blow."

COLISEUM

HOTEL AND COTTAGE RATES—All hotels at Cedar Point are conducted on the European plan. Rates here quoted are for rooms only; difference in price being governed by desirability, size and location.

THE BREAKERS—One person occupying room, $1.50 to $2.50 per day; week, $7, $10, and $12. Two persons occupying same room, $2.50 to $3.50 per day; week, $10, $14, and $18.

WHITE HOUSE—One person occupying room, $1 and $1.50 per day; week, $5, $7, and $10. Two persons, $1.50 and $2 per day; week, $8, $10, and $12.

All cottages are nicely furnished and equipped with electric light and sanitary plumbing. Rental includes beds, linen, ice, and water service. Cottages are not supplied with stove or cooking utensils. RATES, three room cottage, per week, $15; per month, $50; per season, $150. Five room cottage per week, $20; per month, $70; per season, $200.

For information of any nature address G. A. BOECKLING, President and General Manager, The Cedar Point Resort Co., Sandusky, Ohio, U. S. A.

AMUSEMENT CIRCLE

CEDAR POINT HAS three palatial steamers, giving delightful steamboat rides from Sandusky to Cedar Point.

Magnificent and well equipped hotels.

Fourteen hundred acres of beautiful virgin forest.

Three miles of picturesque, romantic island-studded Lagoons for boating.

A large Convention Auditorium.

Accommodations for Ten Thousand People in its great Dining Rooms, Buffets and Lunch Rooms.

Miles of shady walks and sylvan dells.

Mammoth Dancing Pavilion with Forty-five Thousand square feet of highly polished floor space.

Largest Bathing Pavilion in the world.

Cool and shady Picnic Grounds.

Famous Board Walk and beautiful Esplanade.

Eight Miles of scenic Beach along the shores of Sandusky Bay.

Cozy family Cottages.

A colossal Coliseum and famous Rathskeller.

Ohio State University Experimental Station.

Picturesque Crystal Rock Castle.

Museum of Natural History.

Naphtha, Sail and Rowboats.

Famous Fishing grounds and Lily Pond Cove.

U. S. Government Custom House, Post-Office, Light House.

A beautiful Theater.

INNOCENT, WELL ORDERED AMUSEMENT DEVICES by the score, and every known attraction for

the resort visitor may be found on the "CIRCLE OF AMUSEMENT," among them:

The Scenic Railway.
Circle Swing.
Finest Carousel ever constructed.
Figure Eight Roller Coaster.
Auto Trip Around the World.
Vaudeville Theater.
Penny Arcade.
Bowling Alleys.
Trip to Rockaway.
Chateau Alphonse.
Miniature Railway.
Box Ball.
Shooting Gallery.
Pony Track for Children and Saddle Horses for Ladies.
Mundy's Animal Show.
Egyptian Palmistry.
Jap Rolling Ball.
Wave-the-Wave.
Roller Chairs.
World in Wax.

Infant Incubator.
Southern Plantation.
House of Illusions.

CEDAR POINT'S sole business is to entertain the public and cater to the comfort, health, and happiness of the people. This Queen of American Watering Places is in its entirety under one management, thereby insuring to every visitor the maximum of pleasure at the minimum of cost.

BOARD WALK AT NIGHT

MANY ROUTES TO CEDAR POINT—Railroad facilities of Cedar Point are unsurpassed. No other resort between the two oceans can be as quickly reached from the big centers of population. Fast passenger trains, steamship service from leading lake ports, and frequent Interurban Electric service, place Cedar Point a near neighbor to all the homes of the Middle West. The company's three steamboats connect with all cars and trains and make trips to the resort every twenty minutes.

FIVE GREAT STEAM TRUNK LINES REACH CEDAR POINT:

The New York Central Lines.
Pennsylvania Lines.
Baltimore & Ohio R'y.
Lake Shore & Michigan Southern R'y.
Cleveland, Cincinnati, Chicago & St. Louis R'y.
Lake Erie & Western R'y.
The Extensive Lake Shore Electric System.
Seven Steamboat Lines.

Trains, Interurbans, and Boats land passengers at the Cedar Point Wharf.

DOCK AT CEDAR POINT

ROCK CASTLE

CUISINE the management feels free to cause of the unvarying terms of praise ac it, is without equal. Our wish and aim is everything for the table of the purest obtainable, cooked perfectly and served absolute cleanliness. The capacity of our dining rooms, kitchens, cold storage and the equipment, together with our vast ex in catering to the wants of the pleasure public, has enabled us to conduct this ment under a triumph of commissary ment that cannot be duplicated else where. Meals are served either in the European or American plan at strictly popular prices at all dining rooms, restaurants, and lunch counters.

MEALS AND LUNCHES AT POPULAR PRICES

CEDAR POINT STEAMBOAT LINE

BOATING—Nature moulded Sandusky Bay into a safe, land-locked harbor of immense area offering unequaled opportunity for motor boating and sailing. The young yachtsman will here find perfect conditions for the enjoyment of his sport. A short turn around the point takes the sailor out of the quiet waters of the bay to the more exciting racing course on Lake Erie. The inland lagoons of Cedar Point Peninsula are scenic wonders winding through an archway of beautiful virgin forest trees for a distance of three miles. Auto boats traverse the stream for the pleasure of the more lazily inclined, insuring absolutely safe and thoroughly enjoyable boating for the aged and for children.

THE LAGOONS

THE AUDITORIUM

LILY POND

BOAT RIDE ON THE BAY—The thousands who annually visit Cedar Point keenly enjoy the three-mile boat ride across Sandusky Bay from the city wharf to the famous park with its many and varied attractions. The scenery is beautiful and the lake air of that bracing, exhilarating kind that acts as a tonic for overwrought nerves. The great resort is sufficiently distant from the city to insure rest and is at the same time in close communication with the world by telephone and telegraph, and has its own Post-office and U. S. Custom-house.

YACHTING

Cedar Point

The Queen of
American Watering Places

Revised Edition

Also by David W. Francis and Diane DeMali Francis

Summit Beach Park: Akron's Coney Island
Luna Park: Cleveland's Fairyland of Pleasure (to be published 1995)

Other titles from Amusement Park Books, Inc.

Euclid Beach Park is Closed for the Season
Euclid Beach Park - A Second Look
Harry G. Traver: Legends of Terror
The Incredible Scream Machine: A History of the Roller Coaster
Conneaut Lake Park: the First 100 Years of Fun

Cedar Point

The Queen of American Watering Places

Revised Edition

by
David W. Francis
and
Diane DeMali Francis

Amusement Park Books, Inc.
Fairview Park, Ohio

Published by
Amusement Park Books, Inc.
20925 Mastick Road
Fairview Park, Ohio 44126
(216) 331-6429

02 01 00 99 98 97 96 95   6 5 4 3 2 1

ISBN 0-935408-03-7
Library of Congress Catalog Number: 94-073676

Printed in the United States of America

Dedication

Dedicated in loving memory of
our parents.

Table of Contents

Foreword

My first recollections of visiting Cedar Point are in 1961, during the great Renaissance of Cedar Point. New midway rides and attractions were being added and a new firm, Cedar Point, Inc. was just formed. There was rapid change and growth taking place...it was an exciting time to experience the amusement park for the very first time.

When I think about what made Cedar Point so special then and what makes it so special now, one word dominates my thoughts: Tradition. Cedar Point has always prided itself as being an old-fashioned park, but at the same time, blended in the latest amusement thrills into its entertainment package. This is a philosophy that is still followed today.

The tradition of Cedar Point cannot be duplicated. It is one-of-a-kind. People such as President Eisenhower, comedians Abbott and Costello, Helen Keller, legendary football coach Knute Rockne of the University of Notre Dame and motion picture great Sam Warner are all important people of our past. Events such as Metropolitan Opera stars performing impromptu concerts at the Hotel Breakers, championship boxing matches, the Miss Ohio pageant, a history-making flight over Lake Erie and the Big Bands of the 1930's that saved Cedar Point from the Great Depression help give the park its character. This is the tradition of Cedar Point.

The modern Cedar Point has tradition, too. My favorite modern-day memory is the opening of the Magnum XL-200 roller coaster in 1989. At the time, the park needed a signature ride. We wanted something grand. We wanted something big. Really big. What we got was the Magnum, the tallest roller coaster ever built. It was an overwhelming success and crowned our reputation for providing the best thrills in the industry. Since Magnum, Cedar Point has added three more roller coasters and is now known internationally for having more coasters than anywhere else in the world. Roller coasters have been a strong tradition at the park since 1892, when we built our first one.

In 1995, Cedar Point celebrates its 125th anniversary. It is a milestone I am extremely proud of. When a small bathhouse was built along the shores of Lake Erie in 1870, no one ever dreamed that it would someday evolve into one of the largest and most successful amusement parks in the world.

What pleases me the most in our 125-year history is that Cedar Point has continued to be a special place for families. Many guests tell me visiting Cedar Point is something that is passed down from generation to generation. To me, this is what the Cedar Point tradition is all about.

No two people have researched and documented Cedar Point's heritage better and more extensively than David W. and Diane DeMali Francis. Together, they have devoted countless hours to exploring the park's earliest eras, troubled times, famous people, events and modern days. The result: an insightful, comprehensive and pictorial documentary of the storied history of Cedar Point.

Cedar Point is honored to have been the subject of this project. The Cedar Point spirit, tradition, and legacy are alive in *Cedar Point: Queen of American Watering Places.* I think you will enjoy it.

Richard L. Kinzel
President & CEO, Cedar Fair L.P.

Acknowledgments

In the course of researching this book, we met, interviewed and enjoyed telephone conversations with scores of people who enthusiastically offered their assistance. Current Cedar Point staff members, former employees and concessionaires, Sandusky residents, librarians, archivists, and those who simply share our love of Cedar Point, all helped to make this volume possible. Without their contributions of memories, photographs, documents and other materials, a complete history of Cedar Point would have been impossible.

Throughout the three years of our research, the staff of Cedar Point was especially helpful and cooperative. John Hildebrandt, who shares our interest in Cedar Point's heritage, encouraged and supported the project from its inception. Robin Innes not only endured countless questions from us but also helped publicize our efforts. Others at the park who provided information and assistance include Joe von der Weis, Lois Ann Lawrence, Dan Feicht, Deb Hessler and Deb Barnbrugge.

In our search for biographical information about George A. Boeckling, many relatives of the late Cedar Point entrepreneur provided detailed reminiscences and made available family photographs and documents. On several occasions, Mary Biechele spent hours talking to us about her Uncle George. George A. Boeckling not only devoted an entire day to our project but also loaned us family scrapbooks and letters...which helped immensely in writing about his great uncle.

Charles Jacques, Jr., the editor of the *Amusement Park Journal* and the author of several books about Pennsylvania amusement parks, generously shared copies of information from his personal collection. Included were detailed records regarding the construction of the Blue Streak roller coaster.

Among the many others who provided photos, memories and information were James Abbate, Dr. Nelson Adelstein, Tony Anast, Albert A. Augustus, John Balaun, Betty Baldridge, Frank Barr, Hazel Begin, Rosanne Berardi, Howard Berni, Sharon Berrow, Carl A. Bertoch, William S. Bittner, Mrs. Anthony J. Boeckling, Donald Braziel, John D. Braziel, Thomas Braziel, Jeffery D. Brown, Mildred Budin, William W. Burse, Eleanor Brucken, Catherine Buck, Norman Burns, Irene Buyer, John M. Caruthers, Frank Cavano, Jr., Simon Chmare, Miles Fate Chris-

tian, Dwight W. Coffelt, Tim Dagg, Harriett Danhauser, Harry DeLapp, Jenna DeMali, Charles Egger, Alden Ehrhardt, Sheila Stanley Ehrhardt, William H. Evans III, Mrs. E. L. Feick, John Feick, Mrs. Leo Finkler, Mildred Finley, Catherine Floran, Hayden Fouts, Georgia Francis, Albert Fresch, Rhonda Funderwhite, Pat Gerstner, Gilbert Gonzalez, John Grubb, Dorothy Hackett, Loyezelle Haffner, Mr. and Mrs. Eugene Hipp, Terry Holley, Leonard S. Holstein, Richard D. Holzapfel, Joe Hruby, Leonard Jefferson, Dorothy Keppen, Glenn C. Kuebeler, Karl W. Kurtz, Evelyn Laepply, Van Lane, Irene Leeds, Sally Leizman, Gasper C. Lococo, Jeannette McCarty, the late Bob McKay, Jim Marshall, Janice Moore, Mr. and Mrs. Frank Murru, Dick Mutz, George Mylander, Joyce Orshoski, Claude Peterson, John Poggiali, Dick Posner, Hans Reiss, Mrs. Howard E. Rodd, Mrs. George A. Roose, Elaine Rosenstein, Herbert Ross, Mr. and Mrs. Joseph Santi, Ed Schmid, Elmer Schacht, Betty Schneider, Wilbert G. Schwer, Norman Sharp, B. Derek Shaw, Tom Singler, Howard R. Smith, Polly Smith, Dorothy Staker, Mr. and Mrs. Edward S. Starr, Laura M. Stellhorn, Albert J. Tedaldi, Nancy Jane Tetzlaff, Ginger Toth, Jackie Toth, Andrew Vettel, William A. Warfel, Ray Weber, Ted Wilk, Alden Wintersteller, and Mr. and Mrs. B. G. Zeiher.

The librarians, archivists, directors and others associated with the following libraries, universities, museums and companies were constantly gracious and helpful in locating new pieces of information or photographs: Akron-Summit County Public Library, American Foundation for the Blind, the American Legion, Bowling Green State University/Center for Archival Collections, City of Sandusky, Cleveland Public Library, Cleveland State University, Erie County, The Follett House Museum, Goodyear Tire & Rubber Company, Great Lakes Historical Society, Rutherford B. Hayes Presidential Center, Indiana State Library, Institute for Great Lakes Research/Bowling Green State University, Library of Congress, *The Lion* Magazine, Medina County District Library, Metropolitan Opera, Michigan City Historical Society, Michigan City Public Library, National Amusement Park Historical Association, National Archives, Ohio Bell Telephone, Ohio Historical Society, The Ohio State University, Owens-Illinois Corporation, Pinellas County Historical Museum, Providence Hospital,

Acknowledgements...125th Anniversary Edition

Soon after the first edition of this book was published in 1988, we realized that the constant expansion of Cedar Point would make the book's final chapter obsolete within a few seasons. With this in mind, we continued to collect current and historical information and photographs related to Cedar Point. The park's 125th Anniversary season offered the perfect opportunity to issue a revised edition of *Ceder Point: The Queen of American Watering Places.* The new edition contains more than 200 photographs, many never before published, and the final chapter brings Cedar Point's story up to the 1995 season.

Because the current work is a continuation of our earlier research, we again acknowledge our debt to all of the people and institutions that assisted us in the research and preparation of the 1988 edition. Among those who provided photographs that did not appear in the original edition are Raymond Roop and Bruce Young. The maps that are used in the new edition were drawn by Sandi Hansen and we also wish to thank Sue Rist, who handled numerous details related to new edition.

The staff of Cedar Point offered encouragement, invaluable information from their files, and numerous new photographs for inclusion in the new edition. Without their assistance, this volume would not have been possible. Among the people at Cedar Point who provided constant assistance are: Richard Kinzel, President and CEO; Don Miears, Executive Vice President; John Hildebrandt, Vice President of Marketing; Robin Innes, Public Relations Manager; and Dan Feicht, Visual Communications Coordinator. Finally, Janice Lifke, Public Relations Coordinator, endured almost constant requests for information, photocopies, research data, and photographs during the very busy 1994 season.

To each of the people who helped us prepare this new edition of Cedar Point's history, we owe a debt of gratitude.

David W. Francis
Diane DeMali Francis
Wadsworth, Ohio
November 1, 1994

Prologue - 1918

The June morning was perfect—not yet hot, but pleasantly warm, with a light summer breeze that playfully ruffled the feather on Jessie Hammerstrom's wide-brimmed hat. Jessie, her husband, John, and their two children, Bill and little Jessie, were bound for three days of fun and relaxation at Cedar Point. They even had reservations for two nights at the magnificent Breakers Hotel. The Hammerstroms had come by streetcar from their east-side Cleveland home to the East 9th Street pier, where they purchased tickets for the big side-wheel steamer, *City of Erie*, which would take them directly to the Cedar Point dock. The green-hulled steamer was tied to the west side of the pier, and the Hammerstrom children were thrilled to see that she was already belching coal smoke, eager to begin her trip to the nationally famous resort.

The Hammerstroms hurried up the gangplank along with a thousand other Cleveland area funseekers. Jessie hoped for a calm lake so the *City of Erie* would roll less than the *Eastland* had on their last trip to the Point, in 1910. And, even as the hands on her husband's gold pocket watch moved to 8 a.m., Jessie heard the *City of Erie's* deep-throated whistle sound as the steamer slowly backed into Cleveland Harbor.

Now the children's excitement mounted, for in just a few short hours they would experience firsthand the wonderful sights and sounds they had so far only heard about from friends. Bill could hardly wait to ride the Leap the Dips roller coaster, and he was sure he was too brave to let out so much as a peep on the downhill run. As for little Jessie, she had heard that there was a wonderful carousel at Cedar Point with not only horses but any number of beautifully carved and decorated animals to ride.

Mrs. Hammerstrom was truly grateful for this outing with her loved ones. Already that awful war had reached out to the families of many of her friends, and she fervently hoped it would be over before it touched her own large family. Meanwhile, they had an entire three days to relax and forget their cares on that incredible sandy-white Cedar Point beach.

As the *City of Erie* turned west and gained speed, John Hammerstrom held his children's attention by pointing out Cleveland's western suburbs, then Lorain, Vermilion, and a host of other small lakeside communities they passed. It was almost noontime when passengers began craning their necks and the younger ones ran to the rail to catch a glimpse of that famous beach and the lemon-yellow and brown facade of the giant Breakers Hotel. It wouldn't be long now. Soon they would dock and begin their adventure at the famous resort that had come to be known as "The Queen of American Watering Places."

As little Jessie Hammerstrom waited for the boat to dock, she already knew that she would never forget this trip as long as she lived; and when she grew up, she, in turn, would take her children to Cedar Point. As it happened, Jessie made the trip to Cedar Point many times in her life. And, when she had a son of her own, she took him to the resort as well and regaled him with stories of the Cedar Point of her youth. It was Jessie's stories, as well as his own youthful trips to the Point during the 1950s, that instilled a life-long love of Cedar Point in her son, David W. Francis, co-author of this history.

Chapter One
Cedar Point at its best
The Summer of 1918

It was the summer of 1918 and a million wives and sweethearts were singing "'Til We Meet Again" as they waved their men off to war. Across America, summer resorts and amusement parks braced themselves for what would surely be an unusual season. For the first time in over fifty years, America was involved in a major war. Yet, despite the fact that American troops were engaged at Chateau Thierry and Belleau Wood, the beaches at Coney Island were surprisingly crowded; and the breezy hotels of Atlantic City were thronged, as usual, with socialite and middle class vacationer alike.

Nationwide, resorts and amusement parks opened their gates in May and June of 1918, hoping against hope that, in spite of the war, they would see a somewhat normal season. Indeed, most were very pleasantly surprised by a season of high attendance and corresponding profits. Cedar Point in Sandusky, Ohio, was no exception. In fact, despite the war and its various restrictions, the summer of 1918 proved to be a typically good one for Cedar Point. Life at the popular resort went on as usual, with the possible exception being a noticeable shortage of young men available to work as bellhops, ride operators, waiters and so forth.

The World War notwithstanding, the 1918 season would bring many new additions and improvements to Cedar Point. For starters, the old Penny Arcade was razed, and beautiful new plants and shrubs were planted throughout the grounds. Cedar Point President, George A. Boeckling, had a penchant for flora and fauna; and over the years the landscaping at the resort had become legendary. Also that season, the Grill, Cedar Point's finest restaurant, was entirely remodeled; and a new park-like section called the Girandi was laid out, complete with fountains and several pieces of metal statuary. However, without doubt, the most notable addition in 1918 was an enormous new roller coaster, The Leap Frog Railway, billed as the longest and largest scenic railway in America. Con-

struction of the coaster had begun during the 1917 season but was not completed before that season's end. Built by the Lake Erie Amusement Company at a cost of $45,000, the Leap Frog contained 100,000 feet of new lumber. Its first hill towered seventy feet above the ground, and screams of terror were heard from the passengers each time the cars plunged down that chilling sixty-six foot drop. On busy days the Leap Frog operated four trains of cars, each carrying twenty-four passengers. And every evening after dark, a battery of searchlights played over the ride structure and station, adding an aura of mystery and excitement to riding the Leap Frog at night.

To the casual observer, 1918 seemed much like any other season at Cedar Point; but behind the scenes, wartime restrictions were wreaking havoc. Sugar, a prime ingredient in so many amusement park refreshments, was strictly rationed. Later, coal was also restricted, which may account for the absence of steamship service between Toledo and Cedar Point in 1918. When the Cleveland & Sandusky Brewery announced it would have to shut down operations due to the coal shortage, Cedar Point realized that it, too, had reason to worry. The resort's big powerhouse not only generated all of the electric power used on the peninsula, but also provided steam for the resort's laundry rooms. Coal barges made regular trips down the lagoons to deliver coal to the powerhouse boilers. Obviously, if the supply of coal was not sufficient, resort lights would go out, rides would stop and ice cream freezers would warm. Fortunately, none of these things happened, but the possibility had been too close for comfort.

Another close call that year involved the restaurants at the resort. In May, Joseph Singler, Cedar Point's purchasing agent, made his annual trip to Chicago's stockyards to buy beef for the resort. By opening day, over two tons of beef, worth more than $8,000, was hanging in the park's food locker. Before it could be prepared and served at table, however, the Food

Administration issued regulations regarding the sale and serving of beef for the war's duration. Cedar Point did, indeed, own the beef but, under the new regulations, could not serve it to the thousands of beef-loving resort and hotel guests. Eventually, due to Boeckling's considerable influence in high places, as well as to the efforts of Erie County officials, the Food Administration granted Cedar Point permission to serve the beef during the month of July . . . but only at the evening meal, and only until the current supply had been exhausted. Needless to say, the end of the 1918 season saw some major changes in restaurant menus at the resort.

Transportation to the resort was also seriously threatened by wartime restrictions. Already the Toledo to Cedar Point steamship route, which had been handled by the *State of New York* in 1917, had been suspended, although the *Arrow* ran from Toledo to Sandusky on Sundays. When the season opened, the *Frank E. Kirby* was scheduled to run from Detroit, the *City of Erie* from Cleveland and the *Reliance* from Fremont. Of course, the continued operation of all these ships was dependent upon an available supply of coal. If the steamers stopped running, Cedar Point would have a disastrous season. The remainder of the resort's volume business came by excursion trains from many cities in Ohio, Michigan and Indiana. On weekends they came in great numbers to Sandusky's Columbus Street docks where thousands of passengers transferred to Cedar Point's boats, the *G.A. Boeckling, R.B. Hayes* and the little *Dispatch*. From the 1880s on, it was this steady influx of passenger trains that accounted for much of Cedar Point's growth and prosperity. Before the 1918 season, word from the government indicated that no trains would be available, due to troop and supply movements. Then in June, the government decreed that trains not needed for wartime service might be used for excursion purposes. Boeckling immediately scrambled to sign railroad contracts for any trains that could be obtained. As it happened, the trains never did become available and the railway tracks near the Sandusky docks remained empty. It was clear that, at least for the 1918 season, the resort would live or die according to the number of patrons arriving by ship, automobile and the electric interurban railways. Opening day arrived with all of these concerns weighing heavily on the managers in the Cedar Point Administration Building. To their astonishment, over 20,000 people thronged the resort that day. Boeckling was quick to announce the largest opening day in history, and also predicted that the entire season would break all previous records. Indeed, most of the pre-season specters did not materialize, and after some early days of continuous rain, the season settled down to a fairly normal routine.

Even though Cedar Point preferred to view itself as a resort for the upper classes, there was always plenty of down-to-earth entertainment to delight the thousands of low-to-middle income guests who visited the park each year. Trapeze artists, tumblers, and a host of animal acts made daily appearances on the peninsula. In fact, it was an animal act which led to one of the more exciting events of the season. During late July, Adgie's Trained Lions were the featured entertainment. On July 30, Miss Adgie made a shopping trip to Sandusky. While she was gone, one of her lions, Cleopatra, escaped her cage and nonchalantly strolled onto the crowded midway, creating an immediate panic. One man actually plunged into the lake, while at the Racer, Cedar Point's oldest roller coaster, the manager and several riders locked themselves in the ride office. A group of employees located some guns and stalked the lion, only to find her peacefully sunning herself near the lake. At that moment, a trainer arrived on the scene, declared Cleopatra to be as gentle as a kitten, and calmly led her back to her cage to await Miss Adgie and the next performance.

Unfortunately, another incident that summer did not end so happily. In mid-July a young man of twenty-one who had been frequenting one of the Point's many beer parlors was pitched from a train on the Leap the Dips roller coaster and then was struck by the train that followed. He was rushed to Sandusky in the launch *Dispatch*, but tragically, he died before reaching the mainland.

As the Fourth of July approached, there was real fear that the traditionally busy holiday would not equal that of the previous year, which had been very good. But, once again, fears were dispelled when the automobile garages at the resort were filled by 9 a.m. and the boats from Cleveland and Detroit docked in Sandusky bearing capacity crowds. Even the extra two-cent war tax added to each amusement ticket did not deter the 20,000 funseekers who flooded Cedar Point that July 4th of 1918.

Conventions and picnics were especially active that year, and every week except one was booked to near capacity. Among the companies enjoying picnics at the Point were the Cleveland Twist Drill Company and the G.C. Kuhlman Car Company. Conventions that summer included the Fresh Fish Producers, the Retail Clerks Union and the Ohio Teachers' Association, which featured Ohio's Governor Cox as the keynote speaker. These multi-day conventions kept the hotels humming and the midway rides and concessions very busy indeed.

The war's undercurrents continued to surface throughout the season. Both the G.A. Boeckling Company and its president donated money to buy tobacco kits for American and English troops in France. In turn, the Cedar Point Administration Building was deluged with letters of thanks from the trenches. It was during this turbulent summer that popular operatic star Ernistine Schumann-Heink visited Sandusky as a guest of the Kuebeler family. Wealthy owners of a Sandusky brewery, the Kuebelers were also major stockholders in Cedar Point. Inveitably, Schumann-Heink visited Cedar Point and much of Sandusky's German community joined her. Perhaps this large gathering of her fellow countrymen was the reason for Schumann-Heink's impromptu concert in the rotunda of the Breakers Hotel. The event was long remembered as one of sentimentality and tears, for though Schumann-Heink made a major effort to be patriotic, her emotions were divided at best, by the fact that she had sons in both the American and German services. Boeckling, too, must have found the war a difficult time. Although born in Indiana, both his parents were German; and he shared their interest in his German heritage, even traveling to Germany in 1913 to seek out distant relatives.

At 11:30 p.m. on Labor Day, 1918, the steamer *G.A. Boeckling* made its final trip from Cedar Point to Sandusky and a few days later went into winter lay-up. On the resort peninsula, a memorable season had come to an end, and buildings were shuttered against the ravages of winter. By October, only the wintertime caretakers remained on the Point, living in a large house appropriately christened the "Hermitage."

Upon reflection, Boeckling conceded that, yes, the war had had a definite effect upon his beloved Cedar Point. Some picnics, like that of Akron's Goodyear Tire & Rubber Company, could not arrange for railway transportation and simply stayed home in 1918. A local Sandusky newspaper stated that "War-time Cedar Point was bound to be different in many ways from peace-time Cedar Point." There had been no trains, but more automobiles came to the Point. There had been less one-day picnics, but the resort hosted forty major conventions. Despite everything, hotel revenues exceeded those of 1917; and 1918 would go down in the books as one of the best in the resort's history.

On September 3, the editor of the *Sandusky Register* capped the season of 1918, when he described the "summer girls," whose seasonal descent on Cedar Point in search of potential husbands became legendary.

"A summer resort a dead place in war-time? Ask the flapper from Kokomo, or Zanesville, or Beaver Falls. She'll tell you whether or not it was a big year at Cedar Point."

Indeed, some flappers found their husbands at Cedar Point during that season. Others would be back at the hotels and on the beach in 1919.

George Boeckling and the Cedar Point staff soon forgot the sugar, beef and coal shortages of 1918, and began to look forward to a more normal 1919. But they didn't count on the 18th Amendment. Prohibition loomed on the horizon, and Cedar Point had experienced its last "wet" season for many years to come. The beer, wine, champagne and liquor that had flowed so freely at Cedar Point for decades would soon disappear, although "special guests" would always be able to find a drink at the Point, even during the 1920s.

The war and its attendant inconveniences aside, the 1918 season appears to have been typical of the years during Cedar Point's rise to maturity. In the few decades between the turn of the century and the 1920s, Cedar Point graduated from a popular resort of basically regional fame to one of America's most well known and patronized summer spots. George Boeckling was fond of referring to her as "The Queen of American Watering Places," and over the years he devoted almost every waking moment to making her just that.

The story of how Cedar Point earned her title, rode the crest of success, then fell from grace in the '30s and '40s, only to rise again to the pinnacle of greatness, is indeed a fascinating one. The narrative begins now with a glimpse of Cedar Point's very early history . . .

John and Jessie Hammerstrom in the Cedar
Point photo studio, 1918.

Author's Collection

On the deck of the *City of Erie*, bound for Cedar Point.

Author's Collection

Cedar Point about 1918, with Hotel Breakers and the Lagoons on the right and the Amusement Circle on the left.

Hayes Presidential Center/Frohman Collection

A portion of the Amusement Circle about the time of World War I.

The mammoth Leap Frog Railway under construction, 1917-18.

Andrew Vettel Collection

Entrance to the Leap the Dips coaster.

Andrew Vettel Collection

The famous boardwalk and beach attracted huge crowds by the time of World War I.

Mr. and Mrs. Eugene Hipp Collection

Cedar Point's bathing beauties.

George A. Boeckling Collection

Chapter Two

Before the Resort Era

Cedar Point was a geological and geographical entity for thousands of years before it became a summer resort. Its formation began with pre-glacial erosion, the movement of the glacier and the ultimate melting of the glacier. At one time, Cedar Point was totally attached to the mainland and actually formed the northern coast of what would much later be Ohio. But, by the time of the voyages of Christopher Columbus, Sandusky Bay was fully developed and Cedar Point was a recognizable peninsula. Indeed, until an automobile road was opened in 1914, the resort area was accessible only by water. Throughout the centuries, the shape and size of Cedar Point has constantly changed as a result of the action of wind and water, especially the violent storms that have periodically thundered out of the northeast. In 1838, U.S. Navy Lieutenant C.T. Platt, while inspecting the new lighthouse station near the tip of the peninsula, noted that ". . . the lake is making fearful inroads on the shore;" suggesting that crib-work be built to prevent further erosion. Over the years, the terminal northwestern end of the Point has always required protection from wind and waves.

Because Cedar Point is largely covered by sand, it has often been assumed that the peninsula is merely a sand spit. Actually, it has a full foundation of rock and clay covered by sand and pebbles deposited over many years by the actions of the lake and its weather. The entire peninsula is seven-and-three-quarter miles long and can be conveniently divided into three geographical sections, each with its own characteristics. In the early 1900s, Sandusky area scientist E.L. Moseley described the three sections as the Bar, the Dunes and the Ridges.

The Bar is the longest and narrowest section of peninsula, stretching four-and-three-quarter miles from the mainland to a location called the Carrying Place or Carrying Ground. At this spot Indians, and later fishermen, carried or "portaged" boats across the Bar to and from the lake. The Bar is covered primarily by sand and gravel and vegetation is sparse. Originally,

there were only about fifty species of plants on the Bar compared to four hundred in the Ridges section. At times of high water, the Bar section has sometimes developed openings large enough to allow fishing boats to pass through the temporary waterway.

The Dunes section extends from the Carrying Ground about two miles to the head of Biemiller's Cove. A small body of water on the Sandusky Bay side, the cove was named for Andrew Biemiller, a nineteenth century fisherman and one time owner of a small portion of Cedar Point. Before the development of Cedar Point, this area was covered with underbrush and a series of sand dunes, the largest on record reaching twenty-seven feet.

From the head of Biemiller's Cove to the end of the peninsula is the Ridge section. Only one mile long and one-half mile wide, this area was the first to be used as a resort. The Ridges takes its name from a series of eight parallel ridges that developed from a build up of sand and gravel during storms and high water. The first ridge appeared about 1429 and the last, near the site of the Breakers Hotel, about 1899. The full development of Cedar Point as a resort has eliminated most evidence of the original ridges.

The earliest known inhabitants of the Sandusky and Cedar Point area were Indians. The Eries were first, but their annihilation by the Iroquois during the mid-1650s left the area uninhabited, except as a hunting ground, for the next fifty years. By the 1700s, the area was inhabited and used for hunting by the Wyandots. Traveling to Detroit late in 1760, George Croghan referred to the "carrying place" and noted that there were two Indian villages nearby, but it is not clear that these were on Cedar Point. James Smith, a famous captive of the Wyandots during the 1750s and 1760s, indicated that the area was active for hunting, and it can be assumed that hunting; if not daily living, was commonplace on the peninsula. After the 1790s, Indians became less common in the area; but as late as 1820, James Flint, a Scotsman traveling through the area, noticed Indians selling their wares on the streets of Sandusky.

During the early years, the distance between the end of Cedar Point and Marblehead was only 3,000 feet; and when water was low, Indians could easily walk or swim their ponies from the peninsula to Marblehead. Later, white settlers drove cattle to market using this shortcut during periods of low water.

Although French traders had probably been among the first white men to see Cedar Point, English colonials were the first legal owners. In April of 1662, when Charles II granted Connecticut a charter, the colony's land grant included the property from the Narragansett River west to the Pacific Ocean, which included Cedar Point. After the Revolutionary War, Connecticut ceded all of its western lands to the United States Government except for the 3,800,000 acres of the Western Reserve. The western 500,000 acres became known as the Firelands and was reserved for Connecticut residents who had lived in towns burned by the British during the war. So Cedar Point was first owned by the Colony and then by the State of Connecticut. By the time Ohio became a state in 1803, Cedar Point was part of the holdings of William Winthrop, a descendant of the colonial governor of Connecticut. During the few years that the land was owned by Winthrop's son, William Henry Winthrop, some of the early maps of the Western Reserve were made. One map, produced in 1805, shows the peninsula but does not mention its name. Another, however, drawn by H. Kingsbury in July of 1823, makes the first known recorded mention of the name "Cedar Point." In 1826, two other maps, one by William Sumner and one by a U.S. Army Engineer, clearly state the name of the peninsula, although their interpretation of Cedar Point's exact shape was somewhat inaccurate. Five years later the name "Cedar Point" first appeared in legal documents, so it can be assumed that the land was given its current name sometime between 1805 and the early 1820s. During these years the Winthrops made no use of the peninsula. Indeed, it was inhabited only by wolves, bears, snakes and a variety of smaller animals as well as many species of birds. Once, during the spring of 1819, a transient adventurer, Tilly Buttrick, Jr., and his companions found themselves stranded on Cedar Point by a late snowstorm. The Point was so deserted at that time that they were forced to build a small cabin from brush for shelter and live on meager rations for a week until the storm subsided. So wild was Cedar Point that as late as 1889, a giant eagle was shot on the peninsula.

When Cedar Point was offered for sale early in 1830, it was suggested that it would be an equally good investment for the farmer as well as the land speculator. For the farmer, the 80 acres already cleared for cultivation could produce one hundred tons of hay. And the magnificent stands of cedar, pine, oak, elm, whitewood and basswood were ideal for the production of staves, shingles, posts, boards and timbers. Additionally, Cedar Point was outstanding as a fishing ground.

It was not until the 1830s, when land speculation reached a feverish pitch, that Cedar Point drew any attention. In 1836, Alexander M. Porter sold the northwestern half of the peninsula to a speculator named Theodore B. Shelton, reportedly for $55,000. But Shelton was unable to make mortgage payments, and Porter was able to buy the land back at a sheriff's sale for only $292.80. The southeastern section went through a much more interesting series of events. In 1838, Porter sold this section to Stephen Hills, Jr. and Ebenezer Jessup, two New York land speculators heading the Sandusky City and Cedar Point Company of New York.

Although they had paid Porter only $6,420, they proceeded to subdivide their section of Cedar Point and sell it for a total of $428,800. One investor paid $53,600 for one-eighth of Cedar Point while others paid $26,800 for one-sixteenth. As speculators, many borrowed against their investments, as indeed Stephen Hills must have done. By 1843, Hills and his company were bankrupt, with the title to much of the land not clear. The case moved slowly through the New York courts for ten years, and finally, the Porter family reacquired the southeastern section of Cedar Point for a nominal amount.

Despite all of the land speculation, no development of Cedar Point occurred during the 1830s. It was common during this period for Sanduskians to remove large Cedar trees from Cedar Point for use in house frames and as fence posts. Most of the larger trees were removed by 1850, and virtually all trees located between the Carrying Ground and the mainland were carried away by the violent storms of 1858-61. For many years Sanduskians also harvested their Christmas trees from the wide selection available on Cedar Point. After the Civil War, however, the Point's owner prohibited all lumbering on the land.

Cedar Point's first real industry developed during the 1840s when commercial fishermen found it an excellent base of operations. So many people were using the land for fishing that in 1849, Alexander Porter required that all fishermen wishing to use Cedar Point would be required to pay him one-eighth of each day's catch. By the time Rush R. Sloane purchased Cedar Point in 1865, it had already become customary to lease all or part of the Point to individual commercial fishermen. These fishermen built living quarters and storage sheds for boats, nets and other equipment on the peninsula, where they lived during the spring and fall fishing seasons. In 1867, a small railroad was built from the bay to the lake to haul boats and gear from one side to the other. The cost of renting Cedar Point for fishing operations was as low as $600 per year in 1874, and the rental even entitled the fisherman to use as much driftwood as he required. But this lucrative fishing industry also plunged Cedar Point into its second major legal battle. In 1865, Sloane sold fisherman Andrew Biemiller sixteen acres. The following year, Sloane leased the rest of Cedar Point to another fisherman and tried to deny Biemiller use of the waters around Cedar Point for fishing. Legal action ensued and by the time it was settled by the Ohio Supreme Court in 1878, Sloane had long since sold Cedar Point to new owners, who in turn sold it to A.J. Stoll, President of the Sandusky Fish Company, and Amelia Adolph for $4,500. In any case, the Supreme Court upheld Biemiller and declared that the waters around Cedar Point were public domain.

By the time the court rendered its decision, the City of Sandusky had been a major lake port for many years, primarily due to the natural shelter that Cedar Point peninsula afforded the City. As vessel traffic increased in Sandusky Bay, the United States Government recognized the need for lighthouses and range lights to direct ships during the navigation season. Across from Cedar Point at the mouth of Sandusky Bay, a now famous landmark was constructed, the Marblehead lighthouse. At the other side of the entrance to Sandusky Bay stood Cedar Point's tip, a logical location for a light station. A small section of land was purchased by the government and the light, erected at a total cost of $5,500, was first illuminated in 1839. A range beacon was added in 1853, and the lighthouse was totally rebuilt in 1867. Unlike traditional lighthouses, the Cedar Point tower extended a total of twenty-eight feet above the center of the keeper's dwelling. In contrast to the more durable Marblehead light, the Cedar Point tower was built of wood and required constant maintenance and rebuilding.

Even with these aids to navigation, the schooners *Meyers*, *H.C. Williams* and *Gould* were lost off Cedar Point between 1852 and 1878. Eventually, the need for the lighthouse diminished, and its use was discontinued in 1904. In due course, the light was permanently moved to Buffalo, and the boathouse was razed. The lighthouse and the government pier remained on the property under federal ownership and later came under the jurisdiction of the Coast Guard.

The Civil War brought some unexpected activity to Cedar Point. Late in 1861, the United States decided to establish a military prison on Johnson's Island in Sandusky Bay. The prison was designed to accommodate 2,500 Confederate officers captured in battle and was in full operation by 1863. Because the island was susceptible to attack from the lake and especially from Confederate agents or troops operating from Canada, the protection of the island became a primary concern. Cedar Point's domination of the entrance to Sandusky Bay made it ideal for the emplacement of artillery. In November of 1862, amid rumors of Confederate action to free prisoners, a battery of four artillery pieces were ordered to Cedar Point. When an actual attempt to free prisoners occurred in September of 1864, Brigadier General Richard Delafield, Chief of the Corps of Engineers, dispatched Captain J.A. Tardy to Sandusky to build a ten gun fortification on Cedar Point. Tardy was informed that the fortifications were not only for the defense of Johnson's Island, but also for ". . . protection to the town, and Securing the use of the Bay to ourselves." Tardy's construction included not only ten gun emplacements on the waterfont but also a shot-proof magazine and accommodations for a garrison of 150 artillerymen. Most of the fort was constructed by details from the 128th Regiment, Ohio Volunteer Infantry, who formed part of the garrison on Johnson's Island.

Despite these preparations, Cedar Point saw no action during the Civil War. When the war ended a few months later, the batteries were abandoned; and within a few years, all traces of the garrison disappeared. Cedar Point returned to peacetime activity. In the spring and the fall, the fishermen came and occupied their shanties; in the summer and winter, they returned to Sandusky and left the peninsula almost abandoned. The lighthouse keeper arrived before the navigation season each spring and left after winterizing the light station each November. For most of the year, only the wind and the waves broke the silence at Cedar Point. However, that would gradually change with the coming of Cedar Point's resort era in 1870.

Before the resort era, only fishermen's shanties and thick undergrowth occupied Cedar Point.

Mr. and Mrs. Eugene Hipp Collection

The Cedar Point lighthouse and keeper's dwelling in 1885.

National Archives

Chapter Three

The Early Resort Years

It was no accident that Cedar Point became a summer resort. Neither was it mere chance that it would someday become an amusement park. In both cases, Cedar Point was simply caught up in a national trend and influenced by the economic factors that created more leisure time.

Even in Colonial times, summer resorts were not unknown. Prior to the Revolutionary War, New Englanders frequented Newport during the warmer months and sailed to Goat Island where they dined on turtle. But, it was around the 1830s that summer resorts really became fashionable. Turnpikes, railroads, canals and steamboats made locations such as Newport, Nahant, Saratoga Springs and Long Branch easily accessible to those who could afford the elegant hotels and other diversions. Many antebellum resort visitors were wealthy Easterners who came, not for entertainment, but rather to bask in the social whirl. As many as 50,000 Southerners came for that same reason, as well as to escape the oppressive heat and deadly summer fevers of their region.

Early resorts were very prim and proper, with ladies spending the day indulging in genteel gossip on the veranda while men took in the enjoyments of smoke-filled saloons. Dances, card games, lawn bowling and billiards were popular and sea-bathing was enjoyed, but of course never in mixed company. The resorts of the antebellum years were the haunts of the rich and, while they had little in common with the resort that was soon to emerge at Cedar Point, they were the foundation for the more popular middle class resorts of the 1880s.

The large American middle class that emerged after the Civil War had a small amount of money and little leisure time. Responding to this, smart businessmen established summer resorts with moderately priced hotels, usually on a lakeshore or near the sea. Cheap railroad excursions were offered to resorts that featured lawn tennis, croquet, archery, band concerts, dancing and fishing. Freshwater and saltwater bathing were more popular than ever, and by this time it was acceptable for men and women to bathe on the same beach. By the spring of 1890, the New York *Tribune* published eight columns of advertisements for resorts and hotels. Among the most famous and enduring of this new class of resorts were New York's Coney Island and New Jersey's Atlantic City.

Most Midwesterners who belonged to the new middle class could not afford a vacation on the Jersey Shore and began to seek spots along the Great Lakes that offered warm breezes, a pleasing climate and "sweetwater" bathing. Those who lived in Ohio, Michigan, and Indiana soon realized that the southern shore of Lake Erie and some of the Lake's islands offered an ideal summer retreat. Among the first areas to gain resort status on Lake Erie was South Bass Island's Put-in-Bay. Scenically situated on the little bay where Oliver Hazard Perry had once anchored his small fleet, Put-in-Bay's first summer hotels began opening during the late 1860s. By the next decade, beer gardens, restaurants, amusements, a museum and even an aquarium were in operation. Most of Put-in-Bay's guests arrived in Sandusky by railroad, transferring to one of the steamboats that provided regular service to the suddenly popular island. Other smaller resorts also blossomed during these years, and it was into this environment that the resort on Cedar Point was born.

In the midst of the summer heat of 1867, the editor of the Sandusky *Register* directed his readers' attention to the wonderful potential of Cedar Point.

> Bathing Houses—Somebody should erect a bathing-house on the lake side of Cedar Point, about a quarter of a mile from the lighthouse. There is no finer place for bathing in the world than the spot mentioned. The beach is broad, and the finest and whitest sand; the bottom of the lake is smooth as a house floor, and slopes gradually to any desired depth of water; the lake water is the purest blue, and the "swells" simply glorious. . . Will not some enterprising person give us a bathing-house?

The editor's hopes remained unfulfilled for the next

few years, but in 1870, Louis Zistel, a German immigrant and Sandusky cabinetmaker, launched Cedar Point's career. In July he opened a modest beer garden with a small dance floor. Nearby, he constructed a crude bathhouse and some children's entertainments that included sandboxes, swings and sliding boards. Although there was no pier for arriving patrons, Zistel began operating the tiny sidewheel steamboat *Young Reindeer* on a regular schedule to the peninsula. Each weekday evening, the little steamer left Sandusky at 7 p.m. and returned at 9 p.m., allowing little time for the patrons to enjoy the limited facilities. On the weekends, however, the *Young Reindeer* started operating at 6 a.m., leaving Sandusky every two hours and running well into the night. At 25¢ a ticket, Zistel found that many of Sandusky's 15,000 inhabitants were curious about his enterprise and enjoyed the chance to sip a beer on the breezy peninsula. The little resort must have gained at least modest notoriety, for when the steamer *Jay Cooke* arrived in Sandusky with an excursion crowd of several hundred people, a large number of the excursionists headed straight for Cedar Point.

Late in the summer of 1870, Zistel's little resort closed for the season; and the *Young Reindeer* was used on occasional runs to Toledo and Canada. The steamer was never again employed on the Cedar Point route; and, in fact, there is no evidence to indicate that the beer garden reopened in the spring of 1871. Although Put-in-Bay was regarded as a nationally prominent resort and Rye Beach, near the mainland end of Cedar Point, became a popular bathing beach, Cedar Point seems to have languished. Perhaps the only excitement recorded on the peninsula during that time occurred in 1877, when the schooner *Mary A. Larned* ran aground on the lake side.

After a number of years of inactivity, Cedar Point again sprang to life in 1878, when James West opened a group of bathhouses near the beach. A fisherman by trade, West built the bathhouses simply to augment his income between the traditional spring and fall fishing seasons. Although the beach was reportedly well patronized, there was no steamboat service to the peninsula in 1878; and in order to attract more Sanduskians to the beach, West announced a price reduction on both bathhouse and bathing suit rentals. The popularity of the undeveloped peninsula gradually increased, and by 1880, the local newspaper reported that "Sailing and bathing parties to Cedar Point are the rage." Aside from bathing, picnicking was the major attraction, and young couples found that Cedar Point's greatest appeal was its many acres of natural seclusion.

Enough people were picnicking and bathing at Cedar Point to attract the attention of Benjamin F. Dwelle and Captain William Slackford. Dwelle, a San-dusky dealer in grain, flour, feed, salt and cement, and Slackford, an English-born shipmaster, were the first men to realize the commercial potential of Cedar Point. In the spring of 1882, they entered into a very informal lease with the peninsula's owners, Adolph and Stoll, and began preparing Cedar Point for the coming season. Picnic tables were scattered throughout a few acres that had been cleared of brush, portable wooden walkways were laid across the sand and various other minor improvements were quickly made. A man named Theodore Moore not only opened eight additional bathhouses but also the first of Cedar Point's dance halls. There were even rumors that a hotel was soon to be built, although an improvement of this magnitude would have to wait until the turn of the century. The featured attractions were still fishing, bathing and picnicking, but "Mrs. Derby's fish chowder parties" gained popular acceptance and were available to groups of up to fifty people.

Modest though Cedar Point may have been in 1882, as many as a thousand people were counted on certain days, and one hundred or more bathers were not uncommon on the beach. Although at this same time Vermilion's Linwood Park was attracting crowds of 10,000 on certain days, Dwelle and Slackford could be very satisfied with the results of their first season. They had not created an elegant resort but rather a summer retreat for the working man. As one historian of the 1880s noted, Cedar Point was the ideal resort "...because the aged or infirm, or those with moderate purses can enjoy the bathing, sailing, fishing and sociability of this near delight."

The major reason for Cedar Point's instant success was not its crude facilities but rather the fact that regular steamboat service to the peninsula was established and round-trip tickets cost only 25¢. In July, the steam yacht *Lillie* began making hourly trips to Biemiller's Cove and soon after, Slackford's *R.B. Hayes* operated on the same route several days a week. Built at Sandusky in 1876, the sturdy sidewheeler *Hayes* remained a regular Cedar Point ferry almost continuously until World War I. Other early service to the resort included the little *J.V. Lutts* that landed near the lighthouse and Otto Zistel's sailboat *Favorite* that was always available to carry chowder parties to the peninsula. For the next one hundred years, Cedar Point would never be without passenger boat service.

The success of their first season only whet Dwelle and Slackford's appetite for the resort business; and on the first day of 1883, they signed a formal five-year lease for the property. Under the terms of this lease, the operators were to pay the landowners fifty dollars for the 1883 season, with the lease rate increasing each year until it reached $250 in the final year of the agreement. Among the provisions of the lease was an understanding that Dwelle and Slackford could not interfere with any fishing rights or cut any standing timber. However, they were permitted to sublease the property to hunters and trappers, which provided a small source of income during the off-season. The resort's operators were required to construct a substantial dock, which the owners agreed to purchase for $600 at the conclusion of the lease. In addition, Dwelle and Slackford were permitted to add buildings and structures whenever they wished, but at the end of the lease period these structures were to be either removed or sold to the peninsula's owners. Above all, there were to make "...reasonable effort to make Cedar Point a desirable and respectable bathing and pleasure resort."

During the next five years Cedar Point underwent a major transformation. Walkways were added and more acres of brush were cleared. The picnic grounds were expanded and equipped with more tables, while nearby a baseball diamond was laid out. Firework displays for the first time became part of Cedar Point's entertainment bill. On the bay shore, a restaurant was built and operated by the resort's caretaker, Jack Butts. Although the restaurant's menu was limited to simple lunches, confections and ice cream, Butts gained some degree of fame for his tangy lemonade. Over the restaurant a thirty-five foot by sixty-five foot dance floor was installed and "hops" became a favorite pastime for young couples. For those of a more sedate nature, the Great Western Band offered concerts near the beach.

No one forgot that the beach was Cedar Point's greatest natural asset, and new bathhouses were constructed on the bay shore and along the lake. In the bathhouses, the operators offered the latest styles in East Coast swimwear for a 25¢ rental fee. And, since mixed bathing still made some patrons uneasy, screens were erected from the bathhouses to the water so that ladies could have the option of bathing in privacy.

During some seasons Dwelle and Slackford spent as much as $3,000 for improvements, a tidy sum in the 1880s. These improvements, combined with the fact that a leading competitor, Lakeside, was closed on Sundays for religious reasons, resulted in healthy dividends. Railroad excursions brought thousands of people from Toledo and other cities; and it is apparent that news of the resort's virtues was spreading rapidly across Ohio and into nearby states. These excursions, coupled with the local Sandusky trade, were more than the steamer *Hayes* could handle; and at various times, the steamers *H.B. Wilson, Sakie, Sheperd, Jay Cooke,* and *Louise* were chartered to assist. Privately owned sailboats and rowboats also descended on the resort, and these boats were always welcome at the main dock after paying a small docking fee. On one July 4th, thirty-one private sailboats were counted at

the dock and other boats tried to avoid the docking fees by landing at more secluded parts of the peninsula. To discourage this, a beach patrol was established and trespassers were warned to either pay or leave.

Cedar Point was still a small resort with limited facilities, but in the imagination of the editor of the Sandusky *Weekly Journal*, it was a wonderland. "Coney Island and Long Branch present no better, with the exception of immense hotels, and they are not needed here." He could not have known that a generation later the hotels of Cedar Point would be every bit as immense as those of the East Coast resorts.

At the close of the 1887 season, the five-year lease held by Dwelle and Slackford came to an end. Chronically ill and often bedridden, Captain Slackford's continued involvement in the resort was out of the question, but Benjamin Dwelle was anxious to continue a profitable venture. The lease was not renewed and instead, Dwelle, along with Louis Adolph, Adam Stoll, Jacob Kuebeler and Charles Baetz agreed to form a company that would have larger financial resources at its disposal for future expansion. The resultant Cedar Point Pleasure Resort Company was a natural partnership for the operation of a resort. Dwelle, of course, knew how to operate a resort, while Adolph and Stoll owned the land. Kuebeler, Sandusky's well known brewery owner, could supply all of the resort's beer while also adding financial strength. Baetz, although a beer bottler by trade, was a respected musician and bandmaster, whose knowledge of entertainment was of major value. As a group, they formed a seemingly ideal and harmonious management team. At the same time that they formed the resort company, these five men also incorporated the Cedar Point Steamboat Company. Not only would this new company own and operate the *Hayes*, but it would also purchase or charter additional vessels needed for the resort route.

Somewhat surprisingly, it was Charles Baetz, not Dwelle, who was elected General Manager of Cedar Point for the 1888 season. To many, Baetz may have seemed an unlikely choice, for his business experience was mostly limited to bottling beer and the retailing of cigars and tobacco in Sandusky. But as a musician, he may have been unexcelled in the city. In 1867, Baetz had founded the Great Western Band, and for years he served as both director and solo cornetist. In addition to managing the Biemiller Opera House, he was also an officer of a popular German Singing Society. In a city with a large German population, Baetz' German ancestry and involvement in singing societies made him immensely popular.

The new company wasted little time in planning for the 1888 season; and on a cold January day, Toledo architect D. L. Stine arrived in Sandusky for a meeting with the five resort owners. Tucked under Stine's arm were the blueprints for an ambitious new project. The Grand Pavilion became one of the most enduring structures at Cedar Point and its most magnificent until the Breakers Hotel was built in 1905. Almost a hundred years later, the Grand Pavilion is still standing, despite numerous alterations and the removal of its central cupola.

Sandusky contractor A.G. Fettel completed the Grand Pavilion in time for the season's opening, and the sight of its Gothic vastness stirred amazement in those who had known only the tiny buildings that had dotted Cedar Point in previous seasons. Only yards from the bathing beach and facing the lake, the Grand Pavilion was a two-story building equipped with a tall, open observation tower. The entire building was 110 feet wide and 168 feet long, surrounded on three sides by porches twelve feet wide. On these broad porches, chairs and tables afforded guests many pleasant hours of gossiping, beer drinking and just relaxing. As originally built, the main floor was a cavernous hall with a theatrical stage at one end. Around the perimeter of this main hall were the balconies of the second floor that provided additional seating for concerts and plays.

The great new building, however, was much more than a massive theatre and concert hall. At one end of the building was a photographer's studio, a line of bowling alleys, a massive saloon, a fully-equipped kitchen and cold storage facilities. Throughout the structure, multi-colored windows of softly tinted cathedral glass admitted the sun's rays by day, and at night the main hall was illuminated by twenty-four chandeliers. Each of these chandeliers was equipped with three gas jets that were supplied from a gas generating plant constructed a safe distance from the pavilion. Near the plant a pump was installed to filter lake water destined for the new 10,000 gallon water tank. For the first time, the resort had both a large freshwater supply and an efficient and modern means of illumination.

Between the new pavilion and the beach a "Music Pavilion" large enough to seat a sixty-piece band or orchestra was built in anticipation of expanded entertainment events. For the gentle sex, a "Ladies' Pavilion" was added between the new pavilion and the bathhouses. While the noisy Grand Pavilion was designed to cater to the serious drinkers, the more refined Ladies' Pavilion featured a large soda water bar, as well as a light offering of cakes, fruits, ice cream and summer beverages.

The opening day of the 1888 season brought curious crowds so large that the steamer *I.M. Weston* was chartered to assist the *Hayes*. Despite the sparkle of the new pavilion, most of these patrons came to enjoy attractions that were wholesome and simple. In addition to the always popular bathing and the music in the Grand Pavilion, baseball and football contests, lawn tennis, a shooting gallery, a merry-go-round and the picnic grounds were the main diversions. Those wishing to enjoy an afternoon on the bay or the lake could rent a rowboat or sailboat at Zistel's boathouse, though private boats were no longer welcome at the resort dock without Baetz' authorization. According to Baetz, parties arriving in private boats had been responsible for a great deal of vandalism, but it is more likely that the steamboat company objected to revenues lost when private boats were permitted to carry patrons to the resort. The man-made attractions of Cedar Point were very much complemented by the natural beauty of the peninsula. Throughout the resort grounds grew wild roses, morning glories, geraniums, blackberries, grapes, hops and uncountable numbers of huge shade trees. An ornamental lily pond, located where the lagoons now flow, was filled with water lilies in white and rich hues of yellow and red.

Although vaudeville shows had become legitimate and proper by the mid-1880s, Baetz showed an inclination to offer more sophisticated entertainment. In addition to concert bands and operatic vocalists, the production of Gilbert and Sullivan's *Mikado* reflected Baetz' musical tastes. At the same time, however, he was enough of a showman to include in the resort's entertainments such curiosities as a genuine woolly horse, allegedly the only horse in the entire world sporting eight inch hair over its body. This blending of the sophisticated musical theatre and the circus sideshow was typical of most late nineteenth century summer resorts.

By 1890, Cedar Point was being called the "Coney Island of the West," although Ohio Grove near Cincinnati had adopted the same nickname. Neither location was particularly similar to Coney Island, but Cedar Point's expansion program had gained it a spreading reputation. A poem of 1895, asked "Who has not heard of Cedar Point—Lake Erie's Eden Spot?" Cleveland newspapers began referring to Cedar Point as one of Ohio's leading resorts, and Toledo officials had started complaining that the Sandusky facility was so enticing that it was drawing huge crowds away from Toledo resorts.

The popularity of Cedar Point in the early 1890s was a direct result of the constant additions and improvements that Baetz and his partners provided. The resort's first electricity was switched on during these years when the company installed a new Brush Electric Dynamo. Not only did the dynamo provide power for twenty arc lights placed around the grounds, but it also operated an ice cream plant and ice crushing machines. Later, the resort's electrical system was improved and electric light bulbs replaced gas lights in the buildings. On the beach, diving platforms, a trapeze, horizontal bars and bicycle boats were added.

Most impressive, however, was the new water toboggan that allowed bathers to ascend a roller coaster-like structure, sit on a small water sled and glide down a long incline into the breakers of Lake Erie.

Elsewhere on the peninsula, a new boathouse with breeze-swept verandas was constructed. New bowling alleys and larger restrooms appeared. Max Stenzel opened Cedar Point's first "Candy Pagoda" and sold a tasty assortment of cream candy, peanuts, popcorn and confections. Throughout the resort grounds attractive floral displays were planted, the most impressive being a large mound of flowers that spelled "Cedar Point."

Cedar Point was fast becoming a fully-equipped resort, but the most noticeable harbinger of the future was the installation of the resort's first roller coaster in 1892. In that year, the roller coaster was an exciting curiosity, for the first such ride had been built only eight years before at Coney Island. The builder of the New York ride, L.A. Thompson, was probably also the designer of Cedar Point's new attraction. Although slow by later standards, the Switchback Railway was a seemingly daring ride that featured a pair of mildly undulating tracks. Since the Switchback was purely a gravity ride with no method of hoisting a car up a hill, the passengers climbed a series of stairways leading to the elevated boarding station. There they sat in a small car that was pushed out of the station and ran down the series of gentle hills to the end of the course. At that point, the car was "switched back" to the other track for the return trip. Often the cars did not have enough momentum to complete the trip and young boys or horses were used to push or pull the car back to the station. Soon the Switchback Railways were eclipsed by more modern coasters and most, including the one at Cedar Point, did not last for too many seasons. In the early 1890s, however, they were outstanding attractions.

Until the 1890s, the resort management had made little attempt to establish a first-rate restaurant. During these years, however, the bowling alleys in the Grand Pavilion were removed and a restaurant seating 250 guests was constructed. Although a full course meal could be purchased for as little as 25¢, most resort guests were more interested in the well-stocked saloons. In 1894, the management introduced a new drink called "Waldmeister." A locally produced concoction of Catawba wine and an herb that was found on the peninsula, this unique drink was extremely popular for a few seasons. And, if resort guests did not consume enough beer and liquor on the peninsula, they could row out into the bay where an enterprising saloonkeeper seeking to avoid license fees had anchored a floating saloon. Much to the displeasure of Manager Baetz, this floating saloon lasted for a few seasons before the police ended its illegal operation.

The blossoming of Cedar Point's physical plant was mirrored by an effort to enhance the entertainment bill. The Great Western Band, often under the baton of Baetz, when his schedule permitted, was the centerpiece of the musical diversions. On weekends and holidays, the band was usually augmented by operatic sopranos such as Ella Caldwell. On the lighter side, Bob, the "Champion Somersault Dog of the World," jumped rope, played leap frog and performed other tricks. Finally, the universal appeal of vaudeville forced Baetz to start booking acts, and many of the resort's early vaudeville shows were presented on a wooden platform between the Grand Pavilion and the beach. Boat races, firework displays, balloon ascensions and parachute leaps completed the resort's attractions.

As Cedar Point's notoriety spread through newspapers and by word-of-mouth, the number of railroad excursions that arrived from Michigan, Indiana, and scores of Ohio cities doubled and even tripled. The demands placed on the steamer *Hayes* to ferry all of these excursions to the resort became so great that in 1891 the *A. Wehrle, Jr.* was added to the fleet. Similar in appearance to the *Hayes*, the two-year old *Wehrle* remained part of the Cedar Point fleet for twenty-five years. But even the purchase of the *Wehrle* did not relieve the transportation problems that a successful business produced and in most years additional steamboats had to be chartered. Boats also started arriving from other cities, although those actually landing at the resort were limited by the size of the pier and depth of the water. Yachting parties arrived from Cleveland and Detroit; and in 1893, the *Col. Bartlett* gave irregular service from Fremont. Occasionally, specially chartered boats docked at the resort, as did the *Riverside* when she was engaged in 1895, to carry three hundred businessmen from Lorain to Cedar Point.

The success that Cedar Point enjoyed with one-day excursions enticed Baetz to search for larger and more prestigious events. In 1891, when it was learned that the location for the Ohio Democratic Convention was under consideration, the resort's management actively solicited the event. If necessary, they stated, they would erect temporary canvas buildings and install telegraph connections with the mainland. But, in the end, the lack of a hotel on the peninsula cost them the business.

Despite all of Cedar Point's improvements and the fact that daily crowds sometimes exceeded 6,000, competition from other nearby resorts remained fierce. In addition to yearly competition from Lakeside, Put-in-Bay, Linwood Park, Ruggles Beach and Shadduck's Grove, the Stang Brewing Company was talking about constructing a resort designed to compete directly with Cedar Point. Stang's plan did not materialize, but in 1894, a new and aggressive resort emerged on

Johnson's Island. Located in Sandusky Bay and within sight of Cedar Point's patrons, Johnson's Island lacked a sandy bathing beach but was otherwise blessed with attractive natural surroundings. During its initial season, the island was able to boast of little more than canvas shelters and oil lamps, but soon a large pavilion, assorted resort buildings and an electric light plant were installed. Not only did the Johnson's Island management become more aggressive than Baetz and his partners, but they also became better promoters. At a time when Baetz was still content to present the local Great Western Band, Johnson's Island was booking nationally acclaimed concert organizations such as the Iowa State Band and Frederick Innes' Band. Establishing a steamboat fleet that sailed from a pier very near that of the Cedar Point Company, the Johnson's Island firm became most successful in drawing large crowds away from Cedar Point and diverting them to the island.

When the 1896 season opened, Lewis Lea's Columbus Avenue jewelry store displayed a small diorama of Cedar Point, complete with a merry-go-round and beach sand. As interesting as this display may have been to passersby, Cedar Point needed more than this feeble promotion effort to counter the inroads made by Johnson's Island. At a time when advertising, special promotions and an imaginative entertainment bill might have given Cedar Point the competitive edge, the resort's management seemed incapable of action. After the mid-1890s, few improvements or additions were made. Dances were offered on only two days of each week. At times, only one of the resort's steamers was needed to handle the crowds. After more than a decade of unbelievable prosperity, Cedar Point was in the midst of a crisis.

The *J. V. Lutts*, one of the early passenger steamers on the Sandusky-to-Cedar Point route.

Institute for Great Lakes Research, Bowling Green State University

Shady groves made an ideal campground during the 1880s and 1890s.

Hayes Presidential Center/Frohman Collection

The resort's bathhouse of the 1880s.
Hayes Presidential Center/Frohman Collection

Guests arriving at the resort's pier before 1900.

Hayes Presidential Center/Frohman Collection

When it opened in 1888, the Grand Pavilion was the center of resort activities and the largest building on the peninsula.

Hayes Presidential Center/Frohman Collection

The dining room in the Grand Pavilion was the resort's first large restaurant.

Hayes Presidential Center/Frohman Collection

The Ladies' Pavilion, located near the Grand Pavilion, provided refreshments suitable for ladies and children.

Hayes Presidential Center/Frohman Collection

Sandusky's Great Western Band was the resort's main musical attraction throughout the 1880s and 1890s.

Hayes Presidential Center/
Frohman Collection

Neat boardwalks, floral displays and picnic groves were important resort features in the 1890s.

Hayes Presidential Center/Frohman Collection

Photos taken at Bishop's Gallery were prized souvenirs of Cedar Point's early years.

Hayes Presidential Center/ Frohman Collection

The steamer *R. B. Hayes* was used on the Sandusky-to-Cedar Point route from 1882 until World War I.

Great Lakes Historical Society

The art of the sand sculptor was a common sight along the Cedar Point beach during the 1890s.

Hayes Presidential Center/Frohman Collection

The Water Toboggan was located on the beach from 1890 until the early 1900s.

Hayes Presidential Center/Frohman Collection

Cedar Point's first roller coaster, the Switchback Railway, was located between the Grand Pavilion and the beach.

Author's Collection

Boardwalks leading past the Grand Pavilion and to the beach, 1890s.

Hayes Presidential Center/Frohman Collection

Military encampments were popular at Cedar Point in the years before 1900. Here, Company D, 8th Ohio Volunteer Infantry poses in front of the Grand Pavilion.

Hayes Presidential Center/Frohman Collection

The steamer *A. Wehrle, Jr.* was built in 1889 and began service to Cedar Point two years later.

Great Lakes Historical Society

The veranda of the Grand Pavilion provided an outstanding view of the beach and the lake.

Cedar Point Archives

The steamer *Young Reindeer* was the first vessel to maintain regular service to the resort.

Cedar Point Archives

Linwood Park, east of Cedar Point, offered an excellent beach, a bath house and various other recreational facilities around 1900.

Authors' Collection

Cedar Point's early pier came complete with a ticket booth that appears to have been a salvaged steamship wheel house.

Cedar Point Archives

Militia units from Ohio, Michigan and Indiana found Cedar Point to be an ideal location for encampments that combined serious drilling with a good deal of fun.

Hayes Presidential Center/Frohman Collection

Put-in-Bay was one of Cedar Point's major competitors, especially after the construction of the mammoth Hotel Victory in 1892.

Authors' Collection

Chapter Four
The Arrival of George A. Boeckling

The summer season of 1897 ended in disaster for the fledgling resort on Johnson's Island. In August, a spectator was killed by the accidental discharge of a starting gun at a balloon ascension. This unfortunate incident resulted in a lawsuit that could easily have crippled the struggling resort. But before the suit could be brought before a judge, the resort's main pavilion was destroyed in a spectacular fire. Without the financial backing necessary to rebuild, Cedar Point's primary competition ceased to exist.

The demise of Johnson's Island was welcome news for the operators of Cedar Point, but the competition between the neighboring resorts had been costly. The decade-long prosperity that Cedar Point had enjoyed under Baetz' management came to an end in 1897, when the company reluctantly admitted that it had suffered a $7,500 loss. Although many factors may have contributed to this loss, the rising popularity of Johnson's Island was the primary one. And Cedar Point seemed content to admit that Johnson's Island was its equal. When a bicycle race was proposed between the championship lady racers from both resorts, Cedar Point's management casually permitted the popular event to be held at the Johnson's Island resort.

The competition from Johnson's Island and the resulting loss of revenue manifested itself in some very visible ways at Cedar Point. The buildings were poorly maintained, and all were dirty and in need of paint. The landscaping was neglected, and the famous boardwalk fell into disrepair. In the bathhouse, hundreds of bathing suits were worn and in need of replacement.

The depressed financial condition of the Cedar Point Resort Company worsened soon after the 1897 season closed, when it was learned that one of the owners, B.F. Dwelle, had defaulted on loan payments to a local bank. In order to obtain the loan four years earlier, Dwelle had used his one-fifth share of Cedar Point as collateral. When he failed to make payments, the bank threatened to foreclose on the property, forcing the other four partners to pay the bank almost $5,000.

Dwelle's share was then offered for sale at an auction held on the resort's pier in October and, not surprisingly, was acquired by Baetz, who now became the largest shareholder in the company. By this time, however, the company was at the point of financial embarrassment, no money was available for repairs or improvements and the possibility that Cedar Point would not open in 1898 was a real one.

At this point, with Cedar Point's future very much in doubt, a man arrived in Sandusky who would not only save the resort but also convert it into one of America's finest summer spas.

The son of German immigrants, George Arthur Boeckling had been born in Michigan City, Indiana, on February 2, 1862; and seemingly little in his early career prepared him to manage and develop a summer resort. With little formal education, Boeckling was forced to quit school and work as a clerk in a local grocery store. By the 1880s, he had left Michigan City and was enjoying a successful job as a salesman for the Alaska Refrigerator Company, but his boundless ambition led him to Indianapolis, where he founded both a wholesale lumber company and a real estate business. Not only did he obtain contracts with railroads for supplying ties, but he also became involved in the construction of the entire town of Albany, Indiana. Exactly why he arrived in Sandusky during the Fall of 1897, has never been clear, but it is entirely possible that his knowledge of Cedar Point had come from his business dealings with the railroads that ran many summer excursions from Indianapolis to Sandusky.

Although little is known about the circumstances surrounding Boeckling's entry into the management of Cedar Point, it was soon evident that he was to be the resort's salvation. Over the next thirty years, his enthusiastic direction was singularly responsible for the massive growth and tremendous popularity of Cedar Point. Boeckling became a member of the exclusive group of men who, between the 1890s and the 1920s, used their innate understanding of public taste to develop the nation's finest resorts and amusement parks. Among Boeckling's peers was John Lake Young, who became wealthy by developing the great amusement piers at Atlantic City. And at New York's gigantic Coney Island were Fred Thompson and Elmer "Skip" Dundy who built the monumental Luna Park and their major competitor, George C. Tilyou, who constructed the famous Steeplechase Park. Like Boeckling, each of these men started out with little money and went on to create highly profitable resorts from previously undeveloped or partially developed facilities.

Whatever arguments Boeckling may have presented for his inclusion in the Cedar Point operation must have been very convincing, for late in December of 1897, a new company, the Cedar Point Pleasure Resort Company of Indiana, was formed (In 1905, the firm became an Ohio corporation). Cedar Point was promptly sold to the new company for the announced price of $256,000. Although Boeckling may have contributed $50,000 to the purchase price, most of the sale was accomplished through an exchange of stock, and Baetz, Stoll, Adolph and Kuebeler remained major shareholders. Baetz was also retained as resident manager, although he soon clashed with the domineering Boeckling and disappeared from the scene. Likewise, Adolph and Stoll were soon bought out by Boeckling and other local investors. By 1901, Boeckling, August Kuebeler, Jr., Jacob Kuebeler, and C. G. Nielson controlled the resort. The latter was also the owner of Sandusky's Nielsen Opera House, where Boeckling served as manager until 1904, when Cedar Point began to occupy all of his time. Gradually, Boeckling bought many additional shares of stock; and by about 1910, he owned controlling interest in the company, as well as the many subsidiary companies that he established. Through his control of Cedar Point and his association with Sandusky's leading politicians, attorneys, bankers and businessmen, Boeckling soon became Sandusky's wealthiest and most prominent citizen.

With only five months to prepare for the 1898 season, Boeckling concentrated exclusively on those improvements that could be accomplished quickly and with limited expenditures. The buildings were thoroughly cleaned and painted. In the Grand Pavilion, the stage was enlarged and a theatrical artist was engaged to paint an elegant new curtain. The curtain, a misty blue rendering of the Rhine River, not only reflected Boeckling's German lineage but also proved an attraction for Sandusky's large German population. A new merry-go-round was also installed, and in the bathhouse, the old, worn suits were replaced with 3,000 new ones. With America's War with Spain making daily headlines, Boeckling hired Captain Bob

Cook to produce nightly re-creations of the recent Battle of Manila Bay, and a chorus of 1,000 soldiers provided a robust version of *The Star Spangled Banner.* Already Boeckling was capitalizing on current events and public interest. Although he had considered replacing vaudeville shows with comic light opera, he sensibly expanded the vaudeville offerings, booking more and better acts. When the 1898 season came to a close, Boeckling could boast of a modest profit and a gross income of $55,000. These company grosses would consistently rise to $110,000 in 1903, $400,000 in 1908 and well over $1,000,000 by the 1920s.

With more time to plan for the 1899 season, Boeckling began working on his master plan for the resort. Long before the season opened, he printed and distributed thousands of brochures . . . the first of many used to promote the resort during the next three decades. Although Boeckling still had relatively little to sell, he was becoming a master showman and boldly declared Cedar Point "Ohio's Greatest Pleasure Resort." Years later he would favorably compare it with Atlantic City and even claim that Cedar Point was the most beautiful spot on earth. In his first brochure Boeckling noted: "No dream of Fairyland has ever pictured more charming retreats, and one has but to witness a Cedar Point sunset to be convinced that of the sublimity of nature the half has not been told."

Improvements now came with regularity as the steamships, the bathhouse, the camping grounds and the Grand Pavilion were all renovated and improved. The food services tempted hungry guests with everything from complete meals prepared by first rate chefs to the more economical 5¢ ham sandwiches served at the lunch counters. But the biggest change, and a prophecy of things to come, was the construction of Cedar Point's first hotel in 1899. Boeckling knew that hotels encouraged extended visits and higher spending, and he often made it clear that long-term guests were the group he most wished to attract to the resort. With this in mind, the Bay Shore Hotel, also briefly known as Hotel Villa, was constructed near the steamer dock on the bay. A "snug little hostelry" with only twenty small rooms, the Bay Shore catered to those who stayed long enough on Cedar Point to take advantage of the excellent fishing, hunting and boating to be found there. The Bay Shore was an instant success and was almost immediately inadequate, prompting Boeckling to construct a larger fifty-five room hotel in time for the 1901 season. The White House, although still modest, was much more ornate than the Bay Shore, which was now being used as a boarding house. Construction of the White House cost $10,000 and included plaster walls, electric lights, call bells and broad verandas. Rooms were arranged on two floors, with wide porches on three sides. Most of the rooms were only nine feet square, but slightly larger corner rooms were offered at higher rates. Each floor was fitted with restrooms; and on the main floor were a comfortable lobby, offices, a cigar counter and two ladies' sitting rooms. But even the new hotel wasn't large enough to accommodate an adequate number of guests, and two years later an addition gave the White House a total of 125 rooms. At the same time, the company also started constructing cottages and eventually several dozen cottages were being rented by the week, month or season at Cedar Point.

While these accommodations were under construction, attention was also given to improving the resort's entertainment fare. With the vaudeville offering greatly strengthened, Boeckling reviewed the resort's concert band, quickly replacing the standard Great Western Band with Sandusky's popular E.B. Ackley Band. However, due to a disagreement with Boeckling, Ackley's long and distinguished musical career was not to be spent at Cedar Point. But he did stay long enough to write the first piece of music dedicated to the resort, the *Cedar Point March* of 1902. Although this march never became very popular, it was only the first of a long list of music dedicated to Cedar Point. In fact, possibly more music has been written about Cedar Point than about any other summer resort. Ackley's march was followed by F.P. Russo's *Cedar Point March* (1910), the popular song *On the Boat Eastland* (1911), Leopold Adler's *G.A. Boeckling March* (1916), *Cedar Point . . . That's The Place* (1922), Bob Friedman's *Cedar Point Parade* (1964), and *The Breakers Waltz* in recognition of the resort's great hotel. The resort also attracted some major and popular composers during the early years of the century. William Scouton, Toledo's prolific composer and bandmaster, directed an outdoor military-patriotic spectacular near the beach in 1900, and Cincinnati's John N. Klohr premiered one of the most famous marches of all time at Cedar Point in 1901. His *Billboard March* not only has remained a staple in band literature but was also said to have introduced more vaudeville acts than any other piece of music in history. It would seem that Cedar Point had become a gathering place for well-known musicians and performers.

During the early 1900s, it was not unusual for the Cedar Point Pleasure Resort Company to spend as much as $75,000 annually on improvements. Along the beach, the twenty-four foot wide boardwalk was extended until it stretched a thousand feet, from the bathhouse to well beyond the Grand Pavilion. The bathhouse itself was expanded to 600 rooms and was advertised as the largest in the country. A new two-floor dancing pavilion, with an authentic German Rathskeller on the ground floor, provided dancing space for hundreds of couples; and one of Cedar

Point's famous landmarks, the Crystal Rock Castle, was built expressly to serve draft beer. Named after Crystal Rock Beer, a popular brand brewed locally by the Kuebeler family, the "Castle" was designed with turrets and gray stucco walls which gave it the authentic look of a stone castle. Meanwhile, the main dining room of the Grand Pavilion was updated with a massive new fireproof kitchen complex constructed entirely of concrete and staffed by excellent hotel chefs and a crew of sixty assistants.

During these years the first signs appeared suggesting that Cedar Point could one day feature an amusement park. Although no major effort was made to develop an amusement area, a few rides were installed during the early 1900s. In 1902, an early version of the roller coaster was put in along the beach. Built by noted Pittsburgh ride and park designer, Fred Ingersoll, The Racer was a figure eight roller toboggan which rose a modest forty-six feet and featured gentle dips that were slowly negotiated by eleven cars, each carrying four passengers. While not nearly as exciting as the great roller coasters that would be built at Cedar Point a decade later, The Racer provided mild thrills for just a nickel. Also added was a fun house, a large carousel building, a twenty-four inch gauge miniature steam railway that carried passengers on a mile-long journey through artificial tunnels and past tiny buildings, and an illusion show called "Fairies in the Well." Near the beach, a pony track was well-stocked with Texas and West Indian ponies, and not far away was the old bicycle track. In the Grand Pavilion, 4,000 new "opera chairs" were installed, and for part of one season the Manhattan Opera Company was engaged to present Gilbert & Sullivan operettas.

Moving pictures were in their infancy and the neighborhood movie theatre was unknown when Boeckling installed his Kinodrome at Cedar Point in 1900. Boeckling had the uncanny knack of knowing what the public wanted, almost before the public itself knew! The Kinodrome was just another example of this promotional genius. Short, plotless commercial films were available at that time, and Boeckling supplemented this fare with his own brand of home movies. He hired a film producer from Syracuse, New York, to film such local events as the Sandusky Fire Department racing to a mock fire and the steamboats arriving at and departing from the resort dock. By the time the first nickleodeon opened, Boeckling was already a seasoned exhibitor of moving pictures.

Not all of Boeckling's improvements were directly related to selling admission tickets or meals, for he fully realized that the appearance of the resort had much to do with its popularity. Although the peninsula was blessed with thousands of trees, very little landscaping had been done. In fact the deep sand that covered the peninsula made any type of landscaping very difficult. Undeterred, Boeckling imported tons of top soil to cover the sand and planted acres of grass, over a thousand new trees and shrubs, and many thousands of flowers in neat floral beds. When confronted with the problem of keeping acres of grass mowed, he purchased an entire railroad car full of sheep, hoping that their grazing would control the grass. "Boeckling's Menagerie" became something of a local joke, but when the idea of grazing proved impractical, he added goats, pigeons, rabbits and a pair of peacocks and created the resort's first major animal exhibit.

Boeckling was quick to realize that no matter how impressive the resort's facilities became, the business would never grow without advertising and publicity. Indeed, lack of publicity had been a failing of the old company in the 1880s and 1890s. Boeckling hired an advertising manager and placed ads in newspapers and magazines, but it was in the area of public relations that Boeckling proved to be a master. Immediately after assuming control of Cedar Point, he established a yearly tradition of lavishly entertaining newspapermen, railroad officials and steamship owners. Each season these guests were invited to the resort just a few days before the traditional mid-June opening. After a tour of the resort and its latest improvements, the guests were escorted to the dining room for a sumptuous feast of soft shell crab, lobster and other delicacies, all washed down with gallons of beer, wine and liquor. Boeckling's entertainment policies were rewarded handsomely. In 1902, he obtained over 1,400 inches of space in the Sandusky newspapers alone; and numerous railroad and steamship timetables carried information about Cedar Point. Even stories unlikely to be true, such as the discovery of a well charged with mineral water that could turn the peninsula into a major health sanitarium, received many inches of press coverage. Boeckling's public relations efforts, however, went well beyond wooing newspapermen. To entice Sandusky's large German population to the resort, every Tuesday evening was declared "German Night," and the Rathskeller became a center for the performances of German singing societies from all over Ohio. Predictably, Sandusky's Germans became excellent customers.

The publicity generated by Boeckling resulted in continually increasing crowds. Conventions, outings and military encampments were regular activities and daily crowds of 10,000 people were not uncommon. Many of the convention groups were headquartered in the White House Hotel, and the more affluent groups offered their members clam and lobster bakes in the picnic groves. Some conventions, like the annual Ohio State Legislature's August Reunion, brought influential politicians and businessmen to Cedar Point. Occasionally, it was even possible to see a millionaire's

yacht tied to the bay pier.

The railroads were quick to take advantage of Cedar Point's new found popularity, and the number of excursions destined for the resort was greatly increased. In 1900, the Short Line carried 39,000 resort guests; and two seasons later, the Pennsylvania Railroad reported selling 66,000 tickets to Cedar Point. Even the new Lake Shore Electric Railway, which started running between Cleveland and Toledo in 1901, deposited more than 10,000 near the resort's Sandusky docks in 1903. All of this new business was reflected in the fact that the work force at Cedar Point had grown to several hundred seasonal employees and an annual payroll of $62,000. Boeckling had been so successful in rebuilding Cedar Point that, within just a few years, his payroll exceeded the resort's entire 1898 gross revenues.

The resort's popularity and natural beauty not only attracted those seeking entertainment, but also those interested in an education. In 1903, Boeckling leased a small plot of land bordering Biemiller's Cove to Ohio State University. On this site, the University constructed its aquatic and biological laboratory which consisted of laboratories, classrooms and living quarters for students selected for special summer sessions. Since Cedar Point was still mostly covered by underbrush and the waters around the peninsula were undisturbed, the area provided an excellent study environment.

The success of Cedar Point during the early 1900s was, however, not without occasional reverses and obstacles. In 1904, an ex-Cedar Point employee, Captain Charles Goodsite, reactivated the closed facilities on Johnson's Island, constructing a new pavilion, installing attractions and establishing a regular steamboat service to the island. However, Goodsite's venture was not a lasting success. The combination of limited funds, superior facilities at Cedar Point, and Boeckling's determination to put the island out of business culminated in the closing of the Johnson's Island facilities after a few seasons. Subsequently, Cedar Point purchased the Johnson's Island land to ensure that there would be no further competition from that quarter. It was operated as a campground for a few seasons before all of the summer cottages were moved to Cedar Point and the last of the buildings razed.

A more serious situation arose in 1900, when Cedar Point's right to serve alcoholic beverages on Sunday was challenged. For many years, an Ohio law had forbidden the sale of liquor on Sundays, but most local officials had simply not enforced it. However, in the spring of 1900, a well-meaning group of Sanduskians formed the Law and Order Committee and embarked on a crusade to close bars on Sundays. After they succeeded in forcing Sandusky's hotel bars and saloons to close on Sundays, they turned their attention to Cedar

Point, the largest dispenser of beer and liquor in the area. As the controversy heated, the Committee even suggested that the resort should be denied the right to present vaudeville attractions on the Sabbath. Since Sundays drew the largest crowds of the week and beverages were a main attraction, it is not surprising that Boeckling resisted the committee's actions, resulting in his arrest. Following his arrest, the resort's bars were closed on Sundays, although the resort won a minor victory and evaded the law by placing a small bar on the steamer *Wehrle*. The floating bar was opened only when the boat was steaming in the bay and beyond the jurisdiction of local officials.

After the season closed, Boeckling was acquitted and the controversy seemingly came to an end. However, liquor sales on crowded Sundays were so important to the resort's owners that the entire issue resurfaced at the annual meeting of the Cedar Point Pleasure Resort Company in February of 1901. After considering the effects of Sunday liquor prohibition, the major shareholders voted not to open Cedar Point in 1901; and Jacob Kuebeler explained to local newspapermen that the resort had become only marginally profitable and reduced bar sales would make it imprudent to continue operating the resort. Boeckling had already formulated plans for the coming season. The cottages might be opened and rented, but the remainder of the resort would lay idle. The steamer *Wehrle* was to be sold to a company that planned to operate her on a route to the 1901 World's Fair in Buffalo; and the *Hayes* would be operated out of Sandusky as an excursion steamer. It appeared that once again, the end was in sight for Cedar Point.

However, Cedar Point is nothing if not resilient; and during the late winter of 1901, Boeckling and his partners realized that Sunday liquor sales could be replaced with the income from new and expanded facilities. Indeed, the White House Hotel was probably part of Boeckling's plans to compensate for lost bar sales. As it turned out, the enforcement of the Sunday law never really had an effect on the resort; and as weekend crowds continually grew larger, the bitter controversy of 1900-01 was quickly forgotten.

The Sunday bar closing controversy had little effect on Boeckling's plans for the evolution of Cedar Point.

Because so much of the peninsula was an undeveloped wilderness, Boeckling was able to plan improvements that involved many acres of previously unused land. One of these sprawling developments was an elaborate system of lagoons that were to stretch from the center of the resort to the tip of the peninsula. Soon after the close of the 1904 season, Boeckling signed a $25,000 contract with the Detroit Dredging Company for excavation of a series of interconnected, parallel lagoons, ten feet deep and as wide as 150 feet at some places. Personally supervising much of the dredging, Boeckling planned to import a fleet of Venetian gondolas to leisurely operate on the new lagoons. Although the plans for the gondolas never materialized, naptha launches, rowboats and canoes soon populated the waters. In addition, the lagoons proved ideal for hauling coal to the powerhouse built a season later. Cedar Point offered many romantic niches, but the lagoons soon became the most romantic feature of the resort. Soft colored lights illuminated part of the lagoons and tree limbs bowed to touch the slow moving waters, creating a private retreat for young couples on shady afternoons and moonlit evenings.

But even before the lagoons were completed, the restless Boeckling left Sandusky for a visit to the St. Louis World's Fair. The fair had a profound effect on him, and many of Cedar Point's improvements of the pre-war years were probably influenced by this visit. Boeckling was particularly impressed with the classic metal statuary that was placed throughout the fairgrounds. After the fair closed, he was able to purchase many of the statues, and these interesting pieces of art became a permanent part of Cedar Point. More importantly, Boeckling was exposed to the rides and attractions of the midway that included the great Ferris Wheel, one of L.A. Thompson's modern Scenic Railways and dozens of shows and illusions. The development of Cedar Point's amusement section was probably directly related to Boeckling's St. Louis trip; and much of the architecture utilized at Cedar Point between 1905 and the 1920s seems remarkably reminiscent of the buildings of the World's Fair. Boeckling's return to Sandusky was, in any case, the beginning of his most inspired years at the resort, and it is appropriate to view 1905 as the inception of Cedar Point's Golden Age.

George A. Boeckling revived a failing resort and guided Cedar Point's success from 1897 until his death in 1931.

George A. Boeckling Collection

During Boeckling's early years at Cedar Point grass and floral displays were planted throughout the grounds, the boardwalk was repaired and the bandstand in front of the Grand Pavilion became a picnic shelter.

Hayes Presidential Center/Frohman Collection

Cedar Point's second hotel, the
fifty-five room White House,
opened in 1901.

Hayes Presidential Center/
Frohman Collection

The resort pier of the early 1900s was
flanked by the White House Hotel (left)
and the Bay Shore Hotel (right).

Follett House Collection

At the Sandusky pier, on the east side of
the Columbus Avenue slip, a cigar and
beverage counter served waiting
passengers.

George A. Boeckling Collection

Although the Amusement Circle did not open until 1906, The Racer was built near the beach four years earlier.

Hayes Presidential Center/Frohman Collection

The Crystal Rock Castle, named after a popular local brand of beer, was built to dispense beer and wine in 1904.

Hayes Presidential Center/Frohman Collection

After the lagoons were dredged, a boat landing was installed behind the new Crystal Rock Castle.

Hayes Presidential Center/
Frohman Collection

Bowling, which was believed to have therapeutic benefits, was a major resort attraction for more than thirty years.

Hayes Presidential Center/Frohman Collection

Ohio State University's Lake Laboratory served as a research center from 1903 until World War I.

Photo Archives, The Ohio State University

Because of Boeckling's promotional efforts, the beach became nationally famous during the early 1900s.

Hayes Presidential Center/Frohman Collection

Civil War Veterans groups were excellent resort customers, and Boeckling was quick to honor the veterans with a monument on the beach.

Cleveland Press Collection,
Cleveland State University

The Hermitage, the only year-round structure on the peninsula, was built to house the winter caretakers.

Alden Photographers, Sandusky

Roller Chairs, best known at Atlantic City, were a distinctive Cedar Point feature before 1910.

Hayes Presidential Center/Frohman Collection

Around 1904, Ohio State University students could still conduct peaceful research around Cedar Point.
A decade later, resort noise and activity would make such research impossible.

Photo Archives, The Ohio State University

CRYSTAL ROCK PALACE - 1904

The purchase of a fleet of Atlantic City-style rolling chairs was one of Boeckling's efforts to emulate the large eastern resorts.

Hayes Presidential Center/Frohman Collection

Cedar Point's spacious dining room was cooled by lake breezes as well as electric ceiling fans.

Cedar Point Archives

By the mid-1900s, the resort's bathing pavilion was already too small to handle the increasing crowds.

Hayes Presidential Center/Frohman Collection

Strolling on the boardwalk, often protected from the sun by a parasol, was high-class entertainment during the early 1900s.

Cedar Point Archives

E.B. Ackley was a popular resort bandmaster until a disagreement with Boeckling ended his Cedar Point concerts.

Cedar Point Archives

Although Cedar Point was famous for its cuisine, many visitors preferred a quiet picnic in the shady groves near the Racer roller coaster.

Cedar Point Archives

Cedar Point was the perfect location for conventions and many groups posed for formal photos in front of the Grand Pavilion.

Authors' Collection

Chapter Five

Cedar Point's Golden Age

The year 1905 is considered a watershed in Cedar Point history. That year witnessed the construction of the first of a number of massive and expensive buildings that would help create a facility so popular and extensive that few would deny its fame as "The Queen of American Watering Places."

The crowning jewel of the 1905 season, and perhaps of all Cedar Point history, was the planning and construction of the magnificent Breakers Hotel on the lake shore. The idea of building the "largest and greatest hotel on the Great Lakes" had occurred to Boeckling as early as 1902, when it was already clear that the White House was too small to handle the demand for rooms at the suddenly popular resort. His experience with the Bay Shore and the White House had convinced Boeckling that the overnight visitor, who spent lavishly in the dining rooms and bars, was the key to Cedar Point's future.

Initially, the board of directors was unmoved by the idea of a costly hotel; so in 1903, Boeckling considered buying a Canadian hotel, dismantling it and moving it to his peninsula. A trip to Canada to survey the available building, however, proved that moving a hotel could be more costly than building a new structure. Consequently, the directors voted to finance a new hotel specifically designed for their resort and authorized the formation of the Cedar Point Improvement Company. Incorporated solely for the purpose of building hotels at the resort, this Boeckling-controlled firm was just one of many companies established to financially diversify the resort operation. Later, companies would be formed to build amusement rides, operate steamships, sell water to cottage owners, and even distribute electricity generated at Cedar Point's powerhouse.

During Boeckling's first seven years at Cedar Point, he relied primarily on the talents of local builders and architects to design most of his new buildings. The Breakers Hotel, however, was such a gigantic and demanding project that Boeckling turned to the prestigious Cleveland firm of Knox & Elliot. Having previously been called on to design the new vaudeville theatre, this creative firm was well equipped to deal with Boeckling's unique demands. It would be easy to meet his request that the structure follow the architecture of a chateau in France's Loire Valley, but the real challenge came when he specified that there were to be over 600 outside rooms with most having a view of the lake. Knox & Elliot met these demands with an attractive hotel that rambled over eight acres. Most of the guest rooms did, indeed, offer exposure to lake breezes. At the center of the hotel was a circular rotunda that towered five stories above the sand, with the guest rooms arranged only along the outside wall. The center of the rotunda was a hollow tower bordered by balconies that surrounded each floor and at ground level was a highly polished wooden floor dotted with wicker tables and chairs. One side of the rotunda led to the beach, while the opposite end terminated in the hotel's main lobby, the cigar stand, the meeting rooms and various other facilities. Extending from the central rotunda were several three-story room sections, each angled to allow a lake view, and parallel to these were additional three-story sections.

Construction of the Breakers was planned to allow for a June 1905, debut; and in the spring railroad cars loaded with furniture, fixtures, rugs, building materials—everything needed to equip a large hotel— arrived in Sandusky. Boeckling spared little expense in outfitting the grand hotel. Wicker furniture, used throughout the hotel, was imported from Austria; and the chandeliers which hung in the lobby were created at the New York studios of Louis C. Tiffany. The stained glass windows in the lobby were designed by Tiffany's Louis Buser, who gained fame for his beautiful windows in New York's St. John the Divine Cathedral and Salt Lake City's Mormon Tabernacle. Each room, although not ostentatious, was comfortably furnished in the light and airy manner of a summer resort hotel. Large, brass double beds were surrounded by wicker rocking chairs, tables and waste baskets, while oak dressers with big oval mirrors and a clothes tree completed the furnishings. Each room was also furnished with a cozy oval rug, and from the walls the soft glow of tulip globe lighting fixtures helped create a most inviting atmosphere. Every room was provided with running water, and some even had private baths, a real rarity in summer hotels. The rates established for these rooms were not low, but they were certainly very reasonable for a summer hotel of this quality. A couple could stay overnight in the Breakers for as little as two dollars, or they could occupy the hotel's most spacious tower rooms for eighteen dollars a week. The deluxe tower rooms—only six available in each section—provided a magnificent view of the beach and were the best accommodations that Cedar Point had to offer.

As pleasant as the rooms were, the Breakers had much more to offer, including a barber shop staffed by nearly a dozen barbers, a physician, a stenographer, a tailor, a manicurist and even a beautician. In addition, a cigar and news stand, souvenir counter, photographic darkroom and an ice cream parlor were incorporated to cater to guests' needs. Original plans for a huge kitchen and dining room were discarded, and instead a music room and several meeting rooms were added to better serve the growing number of conventions that were to use the hotel as their headquarters. In all aspects, the Breakers was every bit as grand as any hotel on the Great Lakes.

The widely heralded opening of the Breakers Hotel attracted large numbers of guests eager to spend the night in such luxurious surroundings. This immediate popularity effectively squelched Boeckling's enemies who had predicted loud and long that he could never keep such a gigantic hotel filled.

Night after night the guest register was filled with names—from the bank clerk and factory worker to some of the most wealthy and famous personages in America. The better known guests ranged from Annie Oakley to President Taft and his wife who occupied rooms ten, eleven and twelve during the Perry Victory Centennial Celebration of 1913. And, the Tafts' stay was followed in later years by visits from Presidents Wilson, Harding, Coolidge, Roosevelt and Eisenhower. Governors and congressman were also frequest guests, as were noted military men such as General Nelson A. Miles.

Author Sherwood Anderson was so impressed by his sojourns at the Point that he used the resort's setting both in his short stories and in his book, *Winesburg, Ohio*. Popular composer, John Philip Sousa, was a guest at the Breakers each time his band was booked to perform at the resort, but he also made it a point to be at Cedar Point each June to take part in the annual trap shooting competition held there. Sousa was so

familiar with Cedar Point that it is surprising that he did not dedicate one of his marches to the resort, as he did for Manhattan Beach and Atlantic City.

Among the other noteworthy Breakers guests was millionaire industrialist John D. Rockefeller. A youthful Tyrone Power was brought to the Breakers by his mother, who was long remembered by hotel employees for her habit of dressing formally for dinner each evening. George Boeckling was a great fan of the opera, and over the years he developed many friendships in opera circles. Perhaps that is why such well-known Metropolitan Opera stars as Ernistine Schumann-Heink, Nellie Melba, John McCormick and Enrico Caruso often stayed at the Breakers on their way from New York to Chicago for the summer opera season. Many years later, virtually every famous Big Band leader of the era slept at the Breakers during their engagements at the Coliseum ballroom. These famous guests, as well as thousands of not-so-famous people, kept the Breakers filled to capacity season after season. Within a few years, it was necessary to build an annex of additional rooms, and then in 1917, the construction of another entire section gave the great beachside hotel a total of over 700 rooms.

The opening of the Breakers created many new jobs for hotel maids, bellhops and clerks, but it also presented some unique opportunities for small boys from Sandusky. Engaging in a trade called "baggage smashing," the boys met incoming trains near the Sandusky docks and offered to carry luggage to the ferry for a small fee. Once aboard the ferry, however, they explained that the Breakers, unlike the White House, was a very long walk for someone with heavy luggage. For an additional fee plus a round-trip boat ticket, the boys would carry the baggage all the way to the hotel. As a result, many an enterprising Sandusky boy earned a good summertime income without the formality of actually being on the resort payroll.

At the time that the Breakers was first opening its doors to the public, construction was already underway on another massive project—an impressive new 90,000 square foot dancing and entertainment complex which would be known for years as the Coliseum. Allegedly capable of accommodating 10,000 people under its vast roof, the Coliseum was two stories high, 150 feet wide, and as long as a football field. On the top floor was "The Largest Dancing Pavilion on the Great Lakes," with a hardwood dance floor and a spacious stage. Dance tickets (5¢ each or six for 25¢) were required for every dance, and the floor was roped off into two sections. During each of the band selections, one-half of the dance floor was crowded with dancers, while ticket takers were filling the other half with couples. The second floor of the Coliseum was also used for band concerts—often seating as many as 2,000 for performances of Leopold Adler's Cedar

Point Band, the Sousa Band and many others.

The lower floor of the Coliseum contained the Rathskeller, where beer, wine and liquor were dispensed in huge quantities to thirsty guests. Because of the large number of tables, Manager Ernie Michelson annually recruited several dozen college boys as waiters. These college waiters, however, were anxious to earn enough money to get them through the coming school year, and most were not averse to over-charging for the drinks or simply making incorrect change. On Labor Day of 1918, for example, one experienced college waiter managed to pocket over $100, a tidy sum when one considers that the resort charged only 15¢ a drink. Although neither Michelson or Boeckling approved of this practice, it was not always easy to deter the crafty collegians.

The years during which the Breakers and the Coliseum were built was unquestionably the golden age of the summer resort, but they were also the great growth years of the new amusement park industry. Boeckling could not have been unaware of the financial success of such parks as Cleveland's Euclid Beach, Chicago's Riverview, and the huge parks at Coney Island. In view of his love of the sophisticated summer resort, it is doubtful that Boeckling had much personal affection for the amusement park business, but he could not deny that large profits were being made on midways. Consequently, he proposed to the board of directors that an amusement section be built at Cedar Point for the 1906 season; but the board, already grappling with the financial burdens associated with erecting the Breakers and the Coliseum, rejected the costly project. Undaunted, Boeckling suggested that instead of the resort company constructing the midway, individual concessionaires be contracted to build and operate the rides, shows, games and food stands, each paying yearly rental fees or a percentage of gross ticket sales. With this plan heartily approved, Boeckling began contacting major concession operators and thus established a precedent, for seldom during the next fifty years was any midway attraction actually owned by the Cedar Point Resort Company.

A new powerhouse was installed for the 1906 season near the lagoons, so that there was no shortage of electricity for the new "Amusement Circle" which formed a semi-circle from The Racer coaster near the beach, southeast of the Coliseum and almost to the pier on the bay. Fred Ingersoll, who had built Cleveland's Luna Park as well as The Racer, installed an imposing new circle swing described as being the ". . . nearest successful approach to the Air-Ship." The T.M. Harton Company, Pittsburgh-based owners of an empire of parks and rides located throughout the country, installed a $10,000 carousel that was billed as the finest ever constructed. "A Trip To Rockaway" featured a large land-locked boat that rolled and

pitched as if it were on the ocean. In yet another attraction, Hale's Tours employed moving theatrical scenery to provide the illusion of travel. The authentic steam-powered miniature railroad was operated by Heine Gross, a colorful German mechanic who, during the winter off-season, enjoyed touring the South as a hobo. The large midway was dotted with dozens of other attractions including several funhouses, twelve regulation bowling alleys, a penny arcade, assorted games and Mundy's Coney Island Wild Animal Show. So successful was the Amusement Circle that many additional rides and attractions were soon constructed. The original Racer coaster was joined, in 1908, by the $35,000 Dip the Dips Scenic Railway located in the center of the midway. Four seasons later they were outshone by the faster Leap the Dips, a coaster designed by the famous Erwin Vettel and operated by the Harton Company. Finally, in 1917-18, the large Leap Frog Scenic Railway was built on the site of the Dip the Dips, probably incorporating part of the earlier ride's structure. With three roller coasters and dozens of other attractions, Cedar Point quickly became an outstanding amusement park. Even so, Boeckling always considered the Amusement Circle secondary to the resort operation and sometimes did not even mention the midway in resort advertisements.

Although mechanical rides were an immediate hit, the midway also featured some outstanding shows and exhibits that proved popular and profitable. Boeckling followed his early success with primitive motion pictures by exhibiting Edison's "The Great Train Robbery" a year before the midway circle opened. Among the thousands who watched the movie was a young resort employee, Sam Warner. Mr. Warner was so intrigued by the new entertainment form that he and his brother Albert purchased a print of the two-reel film, which they exhibited throughout the rural Midwest. This humble beginning at Cedar Point laid the foundation for the Hollywood empire later known as Warner Brothers Studios. At various times thereafter, silent movies were shown on the midway; and in 1907, Boeckling added a live show—Harkinson's "Fighting the Flames"—a simulated fire fought by a cast of one hundred that he had first seen at the World's Fair.

But if Harkinson's show had impressed Boeckling at the fair, he was even more intrigued by the Igorrotes, a group of natives from Luzon. Seeing the Igorrotes again at Madison Square Garden, he engaged them for the 1907 season at Cedar Point and constructed a native village in a grove of trees near the Coliseum. Here the Igorrotes made and sold small trinkets and souvenirs and lived under conditions similar to those of their homeland. Each night, the Igorrotes provided an interesting sight as they walked in a long line to the beach, soap in hand, for a freshwater bath. James Ryan, the resort's able publicity director, concocted a story which claimed that in order to bring good luck the Igorrotes occasionally made a feast of dogs in a very private ceremony. But, Ryan declared, Cedar Point had refused to provide any dogs, so the natives intended to raid local towns in search of canines. Of course, no such episode ever occurred, but the publicity brought throngs of curious patrons to Cedar Point. At the close of the season, the Igorrotes moved on to the Ohio State Fair and then to Chicago's White City amusement park.

Other shows drew far less attention, and when a Hindu hypnotist buried his pretty female assistant in a coffin under five feet of sand, many newspapers carried the story but the resort's visitors showed little enthusiasm. Of more interest was Boston's Eden Musee, the popular and sometimes grisly wax museum which featured tableaux of famous people, events, murders, tortures and executions. Brought to the resort's midway by ceroplastic artist Marion L. Knapp, Boston's Eden Musee was an off-shoot of the New York Eden Musee and was a permanent exhibit at Cedar Point for over sixty years. Mrs. Knapp, who operated a Florida hotel in the winter, was so successful with the Eden Musee that she also introduced another wax museum, Chinatown, a number of years later. Never for the faint of heart, the terrifying scenes of the Eden Musee constantly drew large crowds.

Despite the popularity of the midway rides, the games, the shows and the museums, Cedar Point's stellar attraction remained its "world famous" bathing beach. Miles long and broadly covered with white sand, much of its popularity was due to a swimming area that deepened only gently and offered safe and pleasant bathing. Author Theodore Dreiser, who visited the resort in 1915 and claimed to have seen beaches throughout the world, agreed with Boeckling that Cedar Point's beach was among the finest. On warm, sunny days it was crowded shoulder to shoulder; and even on the cooler days, it was not uncommon to see 500 or more bathers.

To accommodate the hoards of bathers, a new bathhouse, proclaimed the largest in the world, was built in 1910. Covering four acres of sand, the new bathhouse was divided into a thousand tiny wooden rooms where bathers could change clothes and store their possessions while swimming. At the entrance, bathers checked their valuables with an attendant, rented bathing suits and towels and purchased tickets for the use of dressing rooms. Rooms were unlocked by a "key girl," who also locked the rooms when the bather departed for the beach (by the 1920s, the key girls were paid the "generous" sum of 50¢ a day). Also in the main section of the new bathhouse was a counter where one could buy bathing suits, rubber beach shoes and sundry beach accessories. Another room contained large washing machines and dryers

where, each night, the bathhouse crew washed, sanitized and dried hundreds of bathing suits for use on the following day. A year after the new facility opened, Harry Ward became the bathhouse manager. Well-known for his gregarious personality, Ward was also a strict disciplinarian when it came to running the bathhouse. His career at Cedar Point began in 1898, when he was hired by George Boeckling to rake leaves at the resort. Regarded as "The Grand Old Man of Cedar Point," Ward spent more seasons at the resort than any other employee, finally retiring as grounds superintendent in 1962, after 65 years.

On the outside of the bathhouse, facing the beach, souvenir stands, games, and food counters were installed, and directly in front of these stands a new circle swing was placed a number of yards offshore. Often the riders of this Sea Swing became so drenched that their bathing suits filled with water and embarrassingly ripped open at the seams.

A unique sidelight to the history of Cedar Point's beach was the appearance of sand sculptors during the years before 1910. The general consensus is that sand sculpting was confined to the beaches of Atlantic City and Cedar Point. These long-forgotten artists created bas relief sculptures of animals, historical subjects and scenery in piles of wet sand . . . only to see their art erased from the beach by wind and rain. Like the sidewalk artists of Europe, Cedar Point's sand sculptors solicited donations from the thousands of onlookers.

However bathing and sand sculpting were not the only activities taking place on the beach at Cedar Point. It was also to be the scene of one of the greatest milestones in football history. Beginning in 1905, students from the University of Notre Dame, as well as from other colleges, came to the resort seeking summer employment. In 1913, two of these students, Knute Rockne and Charles "Gus" Dorais, found work in the bathhouse, the restaurants and as lifeguards at Cedar Point. During their off-duty hours, Rockne and Dorais practiced football on the beach and on a grassy field, perfecting the forward pass that had been on the rule books for a number of years and which had been very successfully used by Ohio's Denison University. As a result of the many hours of practice at Cedar Point, Rockne and Dorais debuted the perfected forward pass that autumn, defeating an excellent Army team and catapulting Notre Dame permanently to national prominence. Rockne soon became Notre Dame's legendary football coach, returned to Cedar Point in 1914 to marry cafeteria employee Bonnie Skiles, and was a regular visitor at the resort during the 1920s. Throughout the 1920s, Rockne sent his football teams, including the Four Horsemen, to both work and practice football at the resort. Meanwhile Dorais, coaching at the University of Detroit, continued to visit Cedar

Point until after World War II. So popular had the two coaches become with the managers of Cedar Point that when Notre Dame built its new stadium, Boeckling suggested that it be named "Rockne Stadium."

The hotels, the beach and the new midway were certainly Cedar Point's major attractions during the early 1900s, but the concerts and shows that comprised the resort's entertainment offerings were never neglected. In 1906, Boeckling considered replacing vaudeville bills with comic opera; but his better judgement prevailed, and two daily vaudeville shows continued to draw full houses in the new vaudeville theatre near the Grand Pavilion. However, during one season the resort did engage John A. Himmelein's well-known stock company to present plays in the theatre. Predictably, ticket sales for plays were low, and by mid-season the stock company's contract was cancelled, leaving vaudeville to reign supreme. Although Himmelein's company left a very slight impression, it is interesting to note that one of the company's actors that summer was George "Gabby" Hayes, who later gained fame as the perennial cowboy sidekick in dozens of Hollywood westerns.

Every bit as popular as vaudeville shows were the daily band concerts offered first at the resort's bandstand, and later, in the new Coliseum. After the resignation of Bandmaster Ackley, the resort hired Albert Cook, a noted cornet soloist, to lead the Cedar Point Concert Band. When Cook left the post, Boeckling asked Leopold Adler, a respected member of the Cleveland Orchestra, to assume the position of musical director for the resort. Adler hired only the finest musicians; and under his baton, the band became a company of highly rehearsed and proficient performers, offering programs of popular songs, light classics and the marches of the day. Of course, Adler's own *G.A. Boeckling March* was featured at every concert for a number of seasons, although this did nothing to assure the piece any lasting fame. The Cedar Point Band was augmented regularly by the "business bands" which toured the country in the years before the 1930s. Of course, Sousa's Band was the most famous of these organizations, but Van Dorn's fifty-piece band and the popular Italian bands of Russo and Don Philippini could also be counted on to fill the Coliseum with thousands of music lovers.

Firework displays, which were especially beautiful over the lake, continued their popularity during this era and were sometimes offered on a weekly basis. Most of the displays were safe and routine, but in 1909, an aerial bomb exploded prematurely in its mortar, killing one man and inflicting other injuries. The tragic incident went almost unnoticed, however. Firework accidents were so common that in 1909 alone, 215 firework-related deaths and 5,000 injuries were reported in the United States.

Fortunately, many safer attractions and sporting events were introduced at Cedar Point before World War I. Skeet shooting was a well-liked and well-publicized sport, but for those who enjoyed less noisy activity, a checkers tournament was initiated in 1915, and remained a popular summer event for many seasons. A yachting event, the "Cedar Point Cup," was also offered, but the sport was difficult for spectators to watch, attracted little interest, and was soon suspended. By far the most well-received events at the resort during these years were the professional championship boxing matches that were held in 6,000 seat-canvas arenas near the bay dock. On Labor Day of 1915, Featherweight World Champion Johnny Kilbane made his first appearance in the resort's ring, and a season later he returned to defeat George Chaney and defend his title with a knockout in the third of fifteen scheduled rounds. In 1920, a flyweight fight between Frank Mason and Joe Thomas attracted a large crowd, but by this time Boeckling realized that the rowdy boxing crowd was not consistent with the resort's reputation and the clientele that it normally attracted. Consequently, boxing matches were discontinued at Cedar Point after the 1920 season.

During the first dozen years of the twentieth century, the advances in airplane design and the exploits of the early aviators attracted almost daily attention in the newspapers. In view of the public interest in aviation and the fact that Sandusky was an early center of the aviation industry, it is not surprising that Boeckling was anxious to bring flying exhibitions to the resort. In 1910, only seven years after the Wright Brothers' first flight, the Aero Club of Cleveland proposed a flight from Cleveland's Euclid Beach Park to the beach at Cedar Point. Such a flight required the aviator to travel over Lake Erie for a distance of 65 miles but, if successful, would establish a new world's record for flying over water. Pioneer flier and aircraft builder Glenn H. Curtiss was selected, and the famous pilot was offered $15,000 for the dangerous flight. Ever the showman, Boeckling added another $5,000 to the pot but stipulated that to claim this extra sum Curtiss would have to make the flight in one hour and pass over the Breakers Hotel at an altitude of 3,000 feet.

Girdled with tire inner tubes that served as a rudimentary lifejacket, Curtiss and his Albany Flyer took off from the Cleveland beach on August 31, 1910, while 40,000 spectators cheered. He passed over Cleveland harbor where another 100,000 had gathered; and at 2:23 p.m., an hour and seventeen minutes after take-off, touched down on the beach at Cedar Point. More than 10,000 people crowded the beach and lined the boardwalk for a view of the aviator, who was enthusiastically greeted by Boeckling. Curtiss' plans for an afternoon return flight had to be postponed because of rain and, after a night at the Breakers, the famous flier made an uneventful return on the following day. The flight had generated so much interest that Curtiss was engaged to return to Cedar Point in 1911 to give flying exhibitions. By July, however, Curtiss left the exhibition in the hands of several of his pilots and returned to Hammondsport, New York, to train a group of the Navy's first aviators.

Flying exhibitions, and later actual airplane rides, became so popular during the following seasons that flying boats were a regular feature of Cedar Point for the next three decades. In 1913, Weldon B. Cooke, a man who built flying boats in Sandusky, was hired to display his aircraft and provide exhibitions. Cooke's exhibitions were well-received and he might have returned for the 1914 season had he not been killed in an airplane crash in Colorado. Cooke's place was taken by the Jannus Brothers Company, a Baltimore firm owned by the first pilot in history to fly a regularly scheduled airline. Originally, Antony H. Jannus had helped to initiate and fly an airline between Tampa and St. Petersburg. But, more recently, he and his brother Roger had formed a company to build airplanes, flying boats and ice sleds. They also engaged in exhibition flying and, now that planes were larger, even carried passengers. In 1914, the Jannus Brothers had contracted with both Cedar Point and Toledo Beach; and joined by pilots J.D. Smith and Fritz Ericson, began a busy season of both daytime and moonlight flying. Most flights were limited to brief aerial tours of Cedar Point and the bay, but for 50¢ a person, the fliers offered night flights to Put-in-Bay. Tony Jannus expected to return to Cedar Point in 1915, but being an adventurous and restless man, he soon became involved with Curtiss in training pilots for the war in Europe. Despite the fact that Jannus had become friends with a Cleveland girl that he met at Cedar Point, he volunteered to travel to Russia in 1916, to help instruct Russian pilots in the operation of Curtiss Model K Flying Boats. While there, his plane suffered an in-flight failure, and he was lost at sea.

With the well-liked and colorful Jannus gone, C. Ray Benedict's Lorain Hydro and Aeroplane Company assumed the summer aviation contract at Cedar Point, and for the next several decades the sight of a flying boat circling the resort or pulled up on the beach was common. As it had been a few years before with motion pictures, Boeckling instinctively knew what the public wanted.

Without doubt, the early airplanes and flying boats helped to attract the large crowds to Cedar Point, but it was primarily steamships which transported the funseekers to the resort. When Boeckling took over Cedar Point's management duties, the steamers *R.B. Hayes* and *A. Wehrle, Jr.* were the work horses of the Sandusky-to-Cedar-Point route, although this small

fleet was often assisted by other chartered vessels. In 1905, Boeckling formed the Bay Transportation Company specifically to operate the resort's boats, and that same year he ordered the first vessel built especially for the route, the gasoline launch *Columbus*. With the opening of the Breakers and other new attractions, the *Hayes, Wehrle* and *Columbus* were often in need of assistance from the *Mascotte, Ottawa,* the launch *Col. Woodward* and other boats. Recognizing the need for another full-time passenger steamer, the tired, worn and somewhat fragile old steamer *New York* was acquired in 1907. While Cedar Point's publicists announced that the *New York* was new and palatial, the vessel was clearly ready for the breaker's yard. In fact, Boeckling may have bought her only to obtain her fine engine for a new steamer that he was planning. One of the problems with all of the Bay Transportation steamers was that they were getting old and were in constant need of overhauling and rebuilding. In addition, because they had to turn around after backing out of their dock, they wasted a great deal of coal and time on a very short two-and-a-half mile route. Yet, despite these handicaps, the *Hayes, Wehrle* and *New York* ferried 151,000 passengers across the bay in July of 1907, alone.

By 1908, Boeckling was convinced of the need for a new, modern steel steamer, one built for high capacity and capable of steaming in both directions to eliminate the need for turning around in the bay. In October of that year, Detroit's Great Lakes Engineering Company presented plans for a new 155-foot steamer designed with a stack amidship and pilot houses at either end. Although the ferry had a designated bow and stern, it was difficult for most people to differentiate one from the other; and attractive as she was, no one could ever call her graceful. The new steamer was designed to carry 2,000 passengers, would cost $120,000 to build and would require a crew of twenty-six, including a female cook who worked in the below-deck galley. The old *New York*, with her decks badly sagging, was sent to Detroit where her engine was removed and installed in the partially finished steel vessel. In the meantime, a contest was held in Sandusky to determine what name would be painted on the wheel boxes of the new ferry. While many entrants favored the name *Cedar Point*, it was predictable that she would forever be known as the *G.A. Boeckling*. Under the command of veteran Cedar Point shipmaster Henry Witcher the sparkling red and white steamer arrived in Sandusky and was christened with a bottle of Hommel's White Star Champagne (Boeckling was an officer and shareholder in the Hommel Wine Company) on June 26, 1909. On the following day, the *Boeckling* began an active career that would last for more than forty years.

Business for the Cedar Point steamers was good in

the years preceding the advent of the automobile, and for a while the new steamer ran a regular schedule alongside the *Hayes, Wehrle* and a launch. But the large capacity of the new boat, and, later, the opening of an automobile road to the resort reduced the need for such a big passenger fleet. Consequently, the *Hayes* was sold after the 1910 season, and the *Wehrle* last operated in 1915. Oddly enough, the *Hayes* was returned to the route in 1916, but after the holiday rush of July 4, 1917, she was withdrawn from service and Boeckling announced plans to convert her into a lighter to carry supplies to the resort. These plans were never completed, however, and the last of the resort's "old" boats was dismantled in 1921. For the remainder of the pre-1920 years, the *Boeckling* was able to maintain the route with only the assistance of the launch *Dispatch*, often carrying more than 700,000 people in a single season and eventually logging more than 300,000 miles during her long career.

While railroads and electric railways were capable of carrying large numbers of people to Sandusky, Boeckling recognized that the ideal transportation network would include steamship service directly from Cleveland, Detroit and Toledo to the resort, thereby bypassing the congestion at the Sandusky docks. During the winter of 1904-05, he negotiated with the Algona Steamship Company to establish a daily Cleveland-Cedar Point route. These negotiations faltered; but in 1907, a group of Cleveland businessmen established the Lake Shore Navigation Company (soon to be renamed Eastland Navigation Company) and bought the sleek, fast and fairly new steamer, *Eastland*, especially for the resort route. In the meantime, Boeckling built a $25,000 pier near the lighthouse that was capable of handling the deeper draft and greater length of the big lake steamers. On June 8, 1907, the "Aristocrat of the Lakes," as the *Eastland* was known, made her first cruise to Cedar Point, and that same season, the steamer *Flora* initiated service from Toledo. Two years later, the *Frank E. Kirby* was placed on the Detroit-Cedar Point run; and over the next decade, additional vessels arrived from Fremont, Lakeside, Lorain, Canada and even Rochester.

The *Eastland* was withdrawn from service in 1913, and was taken to Chicago for use in the excursion trade. There, in 1915, she capsized, causing the loss of more than 800 lives; and she eventually became the naval training vessel *Wilmette*. The vacancy left by the departure of the *Eastland* was quickly filled by the Cleveland & Buffalo Transit Company, a well-established line that ran nightboats between Cleveland and Buffalo. By now, however, Boeckling fully knew the value of the route; and the terms of his contract forced the C & B Line not only to maintain the pier but also to enlarge the facilities at their expense. Over

the next years, the C & B Line used their *State of Ohio, City of Erie* and *City of Buffalo* for this service before assigning the *Goodtime* (ex-*City of Detroit II*) as the full-time boat on the resort run in 1925. On the Toledo run, the *Flora* was replaced in 1908, by the *State of New York*, followed in later years by the *State of Ohio, Frank E. Kirby, Greyhound* and finally, the *Put-in-Bay* in 1933. Ten years earlier, the *Put-in-Bay* had replaced the *Kirby* on the Detroit-to-Cedar Point run, and in 1926, the *City of Toledo* became a competitor when she was employed on the Toledo-to-Cedar Point-and-Sandusky route for one season.

Cedar Point's lake pier was a busy place during the golden years of the passenger steamer, for the three regular steamers were often met at the pier by chartered excursion boats like the *Greyhound, Rochester,* and *Theodore Roosevelt.* Since all of these lake steamers had large capacities (the *Eastland* was licensed to carry 2,200 passengers), it was not uncommon for 8,000 or more people to arrive at the Cedar Point pier on any given day. Once off the pier, the passengers had the option of walking to the center of the resort or riding in flat-bottom lagoon boats that were operated by college boys.

The big steamers that operated on the Cedar Point routes for over forty years were not only impressive and colorful, they were also entertaining. The *Eastland* featured a loud calliope on her upper deck, and all of the boats offered hardwood dance floors, a dance band, dining facilities and, in some cases, games of chance and activities for the children. Except in the roughest of weather, the big steamers provided a comfortable trip at a modest cost, and their popularity is confirmed by the fact that in 1913, the *Eastland* transported 200,000 people to Cedar Point during a season that lasted less than 100 days. More than any other factor, the establishment of major steamer routes from the large cities helped catapult Cedar Point to the position of prominence that it enjoyed in 1920.

As important as the development of a steamship network was, Boeckling had additional plans for giving customers easier access to the resort. Although railroad excursions had been arriving in Sandusky since the 1880s, it was Boeckling who exploited the rail services to their fullest degree. He lavishly entertained railroad officials and constantly negotiated for increased excursion service from all parts of Ohio, Michigan and Indiana. Recognizing the profits to be made from excursions, the railroaders responded by adding trains, promoting excursion rates and even printing large Cedar Point advertisements in their timetables. On a typical Sunday in 1911, a Big Four train offered service from Cincinnati, a Lake Erie & Western from Indianapolis and two Pennsylvania Railroad sections from Columbus. In addition, regular rail service to Sandusky was available on the New

York Central, Nickel Plate, Lake Shore & Michigan Southern and the Baltimore & Ohio roads. With railroads offering round-trip excursion rates for as low as $1.00, the special trains were well patronized, and on one busy Sunday in 1908, sixteen passenger trains filled the spurs near the resort's Sandusky docks. Railway excursions became so popular that even the unions that represented the railroad employees began using Cedar Point for their annual summer outings, and at least one railroad association continued patronizing Cedar Point for over sixty years.

With both railroad and steamship service now firmly established, Boeckling turned his attention to the resort's final access dilemma. There were still no roads leading to the resort, and everyone arrived by boat. The first proposal to solve this problem was to build an electric railway from the point where the peninsula met the mainland to the resort. The idea was entirely logical, for the Lake Shore Electric already passed Rye Beach at the base of the peninsula; and in 1912, the Toledo, Port Clinton & Lakeside Railway had been extended to Bay Point, from which boat service was available to Cedar Point. So, in mid-summer of 1909, W.C. Phelps and a group of Cleveland investors, with the blessing of the resort's directors, formed the Cedar Point Railway Company and made plans to build an electric railway from Rye Beach and Huron to the Cedar Point boardwalk. Although they raised $10,000 for the project, no rails were ever laid. Perhaps they, or Boeckling, saw that the future of the electric railway was about to be curtailed by the arrival of the inexpensive automobile.

After it became affordable for the average family, the automobile began to have a profound effect on our society, our economy, and eventually, on the future of Cedar Point. Henry Ford introduced his Model T in 1908, and two years later automobile production reached 181,000 vehicles. But this was merely a beginning, for by 1915, there were 2,500,000 cars on the road; and five years later that number reached 9,000,000. Boeckling could not have helped but notice the trend toward family mobility, and he quickly recognized that the resort and the amusement park of the future would need to provide roads and parking facilities for the auto. It is clear that he was already planning a road to the resort in 1911, although for reasons unknown, actual construction was delayed a few more years. The road, when finished, was proclaimed an engineering marvel of 1914, with a two lane concrete highway that traversed almost the entire length of the peninsula and terminated at a new parking lot at Biemiller's Cove. It was, however, a costly project, for a year after the road's completion, the company was forced to make a special offering of preferred stock in order to service a debt of $205,000 that existed as a result of building the road.

A name for the new road was rather unexpectedly found during the project's groundbreaking ceremonies, to which several members of the Kuebeler family, who were visiting from Germany, were invited. One of the Kuebelers, seeing the beauty of the peninsula for the first time, suggested that the new highway should be given the lyrical French name for a paved road, "Chaussee." The name seemed to fit, and forever after the roadway was "The Chaussee."

Despite the large number of cars on opening day portending its future use, the violence of Lake Erie's weather made the highway an immediate maintenance problem. In 1917, a spring storm destroyed a large portion of the road and subsequent storms caused constant damage. Consequently, Boeckling sought a more protected route, and a section of the road most exposed to the lake's attacks was eliminated when a new entrance was opened for the 1920 season. But these problems and the expenditures related to the road's construction proved to be minor considerations when the results of the new access road became known. On July 4, 1915, 3,000 resort visitors arrived by automobile, compared with 3,500 who came by train and an equal number who stepped off the gangplanks of steamers. Exactly a year later, it was estimated that 2,000 cars attempted to reach the resort, causing massive traffic jams along the seven mile road and along highways leading to the entrance. The parking lots were often filled before noon, and many cars were required to park along the beach and next to the roller coasters. In a matter of only a few seasons, the influence of the automobile was very apparent at Cedar Point; and during the 1920s, its impact would become even greater.

The automobile road served not only as a method of getting more people to the resort section, but it also opened a largely undeveloped portion of the peninsula for residential development. Much space was still available for resort expansion on the northwest end of the peninsula; but the narrow strip of land from the parking lots to the mainland, with its charming view of beach and lake, was ideal for cottages and homes. As early as 1909, the board of directors had authorized the plating of a residential area, and a few cottages were constructed that summer; but the bulk of the area was still occupied by sand, underbrush and a few squatters' shacks in a section called "The Jungle." The construction of the road had cleared the shacks from the area, and in June of 1914, the Cedar Point Improvement Company subdivided the land into small residential lots. A year later, Cedar Point's management was actively selling lots, whose new owners were required, by contract, to construct homes costing at least $500. The resort promised residents electricity, police protection, a ban on commercial enterprises, a nine hole golf course, and finally, a $250,000 year-round hotel. Although a number of lots were sold and some cottages were constructed, the residential project was one of the few failures that Boeckling was to experience at Cedar Point. The golf course and the hotel were never more than blueprints, and the real development of this section would not occur until the 1950s.

Although Boeckling's dream of a residential area never really materialized, his plans for expansion did affect the future of Ohio State University's Lake Laboratory. By 1913, resort development was already encroaching on the research building. In addition, wintertime vandalism required costly repairs to the laboratory, and the resort's policy of dumping sewage in Biemiller's Cove was destroying much of the natural habitat that the students came to study. Furthermore, Boeckling was starting to voice complaints about the condition of the laboratory, the conduct and appearance of the students, and the fact that both sexes were being housed in the same building. He informed Ohio State that the laboratory was welcome to remain on Cedar Point if a new facility was built elsewhere on the peninsula, the students were better disciplined, and separate housing for men and women was provided. But by this time, the bustling Cedar Point had lost its attraction as a collection and observation site, and 1917 was the laboratory's final season on the peninsula. In 1918, the classes were moved to Put-in-Bay, and a year later the resort company razed the laboratory building and paid the University receipts from the sale of the materials.

Unlike the Cedar Point of the 1880s, the newer resort had become the dominant summer retreat of the Great Lakes. Put-in-Bay still drew large crowds, as did Lakeside, but neither had kept pace with Cedar Point's extensive growth during the pre-World War I era. In fact, the only hotel even comparable to the Breakers, Put-in-Bay's Hotel Victory, was destroyed by fire after many unsuccessful seasons. Although there were amusement parks in both Toledo and Cleveland, the nearest competitive midway was located at Vermilion's Crystal Beach Park. Originally known as Shadduck's Grove, George Blanchat converted it into a fully equipped amusement park in 1907. Although the Crystal Gardens Ballroom was built in 1925, and the great Cyclone roller coaster a year later, Crystal Beach was never large enough to seriously compete with the Boeckling empire. However, it struggled on for many years before closing in 1962. And with the Johnson's Island operation eliminated after the 1906 season, Cedar Point entered the second decade of the century with few, if any, serious competitors.

Cedar Point's domination of the summer resort market became most evident in both the number and quality of the conventions and outings that were booked into the resort. Statewide conventions of the Eagles, the Knights of Pythias, the Knights of Colum-

bus, the Ohio Teachers, the Ohio Grain Dealers and others flocked to the peninsula, usually holding convention activities that lasted an entire week. It wasn't long before national groups began to notice Cedar Point, and in 1907, the influential National Vaudeville Managers Association selected the Point for their annual meeting. One of the important events centered at Cedar Point was the dedication of the Perry Victory Monument in 1913. Although the actual ceremonies took place at the monument on Put-in-Bay, the Breakers was selected as the headquarters for the dedication committee. On the night of the dedication, a grand banquet was held at Cedar Point, with noted guests including President Taft, General Nelson A. Miles and the governors of nine states. In addition to these multi-day conventions and events, Cedar Point was also chosen as the location of many one-day company and association outings. Typical of these was the Employee's Picnic of Akron's Goodyear Tire & Rubber Company which first visited the resort in 1914, with 3,100 people. Two years later, the picnic had become so large that it required 130 railroad cars traveling in ten sections to transport the employees and their families to the resort.

Even if the yearly attendance figures at Cedar Point had not yet reached the one million mark, as Boeckling claimed, the massive conventions and huge crowds brought by the transportation network were already taxing the resort's facilities. Because the conventions all required overnight accommodations, the hotels were often filled to capacity, with the overflow crowds forced to seek rooms in Sandusky. The number of hotel rooms available on the peninsula had a direct effect on the size of conventions that could be booked and, ultimately, the profits of the company. Consequently, Boeckling had little difficulty convincing the board of directors to authorize the construction of another hotel for the 1915 season. Reflecting many of Boeckling's own ideas, the new Hotel Cedars incorporated the three buildings that were originally the White House Hotel.

The Cedars was a charming, breezy and somewhat informal hotel of seven two-story sections connected by covered walkways. In addition to 270 guest rooms, the new hotel also featured its own cafeteria, cigar stand and gift shop. While the Breakers had its stylish Japanese writing room and the bustling rotunda, the Cedars offered cozy little corners furnished with wicker chairs and writing tables, summer plants, dark green rugs and softly glowing reading lamps. Many of the windows in the Cedars' public rooms were graced with stained glass creations from the New York studios of Louis Tiffany, and all of the hotel's windows were framed by sheer white curtains that ruffled in the summer breezes that constantly swept the peninsula. Located far from the noise of the Amusement

Circle and from the activity on the beach, the Cedars provided a quiet retreat where the silence was broken only by the periodic steam whistle of a ferry leaving the nearby pier. Combined with the larger Breakers, the addition of the Cedars gave Cedar Point a nightly availability of more than a thousand rooms. But, even with so many rooms available, both hotels were usually kept full throughout the season. And when Boeckling declared that 1916 had been Cedar Point's best hotel season in history, the directors quickly authorized another addition to the Breakers for the following year.

Just as the big hotels were kept fully occupied, so, too, were the cottages and the campgrounds. Although Cedar Point never boasted large numbers of cottages, the addition of the Johnson's Island cottages for the 1910 season brought the total to twenty-two. Some of the cottages were rather crude, with partitions instead of walls, no plumbing, and the inconvenience of black snakes hanging from the rafters. Others were much more habitable with plastered walls, ice boxes and cold running water. In 1908, a three-room cottage rented for fifteen dollars a week or $150 for the season, while the larger five-room cottages could be rented for $200 a season. For those who desired to build their own cottage or pitch a tent along the new automobile road, a small lot could be leased from May to October for as little as fifteen dollars. The cottages were the only facility on the peninsula that often opened before the traditional beginning of the resort season in mid-June. But, early season cottage renters had to put up with cool weather and the fact that regular steamboat service to and from Cedar Point never started until June. While the hotels provided a gala social atmosphere at the resort, the cottage village, located just to the northwest of the Breakers, offered a slower, more relaxed "summer colony" atmosphere.

The evolution of Cedar Point into one of the greatest resorts on the Great Lakes required many "behind the scenes" services and facilities to better and more efficiently serve its visitors. The most important of these was the new powerhouse installed for the 1906 season. The dynamos not only had the capability to power and light the new midway, but they also supplied the power that ran the pumps for the water filtration system, the kitchen's massive food coolers, the fifty-foot by eighty-foot icehouse and the lights in a thousand hotel rooms. In addition, the powerhouse boilers provided steam for a laundry which met the daily needs of the kitchens and the hotels.

To help keep the restaurants and cafeterias stocked with bread, rolls, pies, cakes and pastries, Boeckling built a complete bakery; and to insure a constant inexpensive supply of soft drinks, he built a bottling plant. For more than four decades, resort visitors consumed

a number of flavors of soda from bottles marked "Cedar Point-On-Lake Erie." The bottling works also manufactured the ice cream toppings used throughout the resort...with chocolate and strawberry the perennial favorites.

Transporting supplies around the resort, as well as carrying luggage to the hotels, were logistical problems that Boeckling solved by constructing a narrow gauge railroad from the ferry dock to the various buildings. At first, the freight cars were pulled by teams of horses, but later steam engines, and finally a 1915 Plymouth Gasoline Locomotive, replaced the horses. In the days before liability was a concern, hotel guests were also often permitted to ride on the open cars with their luggage, but the railroad's primary purpose was to move supplies from the ferry dock to the kitchens and storerooms.

As the resort grew larger and more complex, an administration building was needed to house not only Boeckling's office, but also the purchasing, auditing, food service and publicity departments. Originally, a design by Sandusky contractor John Feick called for a classic stone building, but when completed, the new Administration Building was a wooden structure of a design similar to the other resort buildings. New dormitories were also constructed during these years to house the hundreds of college students who were hired each season, and a large, year-round house was built for the wintertime caretakers. Nicknamed "The Hermitage," this building quartered the small group of men who referred to themselves as the "hermits" and who maintained a lonely off-season watch on the resort properties. Gus Boeckling, George's brother, was not only the "head hermit," but he was also in charge of the resort's grounds and flower gardens during the operating season.

The safety of the resort and its patrons also became a concern during these years, and a uniformed police department was added to help discourage rowdy behavior. For fire protection, a Model T Ford Fire Truck was purchased, and later a firehouse was established in the Crystal Rock Castle. During most seasons, a house physician was on call and a launch was available to take the more serious medical emergencies to Sandusky, but the majority of minor medical needs were served by a first-aid station manned by third year medical students from Ohio State University. As "externs" these medical students were on-call twenty-four hours a day and received only room and board as pay. Their reward, of course, was medical experience that few students were able to obtain, and there were always students eager for the Cedar Point assignment. By the 1920s, the first-aid station, like the firehouse, was housed in the Crystal Rock Castle.

In 1907, Boeckling petitioned the U.S. Post Office

Department for the establishment of a fourth class post office on the resort grounds to handle the huge volume of postcards and other mail passing through the facility. The request was granted, and Cedar Point became one of only two locations—the other being Coney Island—where an independent post office was operated only during the summer season. The first postmistress was Boeckling's close friend, Margie Benbow, and the office was soon moved from small, temporary quarters to an attractive pagoda not far from the Coliseum and a postcard stand. During 1914-15, Boeckling and the resort's new postmaster, Oscar Tamm, had a major disagreement over building rental. The argument was settled when the post office became a substation of the Sandusky post office, no longer requiring a postmaster, and seasonally staffed by two clerks sent from Sandusky. This arrangement remained in effect from 1915 until the substation was suspended in the 1950s.

All of these internal improvements were indications that Cedar Point, like Coney Island and Atlantic City on the East Coast, had reached maturity during the years immediately preceding World War I. Although the resort's management may have exaggerated the facility's importance when they suggested that negotiations to end the Russo-Japanese War might be held at Cedar Point, it is clear that sometime after 1905, Cedar Point became one of America's greatest resorts and richly deserved the title "The Queen of American Watering Places." Yet the enterprising Boeckling was not fully satisfied and insisted that Cedar Point was still in its infancy. When fully developed, he boasted, his resort would "out-rival" Atlantic City.

Unquestionably, Cedar Point was not only popular, but also a financial success for its owners. By 1909, revenues reached $400,000, net profits stood at $118,000 and the price of a share of stock climbed to thirty-eight dollars. The value of the facilities, not including rides and other attractions owned by concessionaires, reached $2,000,000 and attendance legitimately exceeded 1,000,000 people during the 107-day 1913 season. So profitable was the resort operation that the company could always be expected to donate to community projects, and when devastating floods swept Southern Ohio in 1913, the Cedar Point Resort Company was quick to send the Governor a check for $1,000. George Boeckling, now the majority owner of the resort's common stock, not only prospered but became quite wealthy. Not surprisingly, his control of the company and his supreme ego prompted him to change the name of the company to the G.A. Boeckling Company soon after the 1917 season. In addition to sizable dividend checks, his personal salary reached $50,000; and he was fond of boasting that he was not only the richest man in Sandusky, but also better paid than the Governor of Ohio. Although he never learned to drive, Boeckling always owned a new Cadillac, complete with gold-monogrammed doors and a full-time chauffeur. His personal tastes leaned toward elegant dining, extravagant parties, diamonds, expensive cigars and the finest clothes. At the same time, however, his generosity and interest in charities became legendary. He was a board member of Sandusky's Providence Hospital to which he contributed generously. He donated eyeglasses and milk to poor children and enjoyed giving children's parties at Christmas. Often, groups of orphans, poor children and Civil War veterans from the Sandusky Soldier's Home were invited to Cedar Point as his guests, and he became the primary backer of the Sandusky Boys' and Girls' Band. To his relatives, who both feared and admired him, Boeckling was generous with gifts, advice and even loans. A tough and ruthless businessman, he was also a great local philanthropist.

With so much cash now at his disposal, George Boeckling set about building a mansion worthy of his position as one of Sandusky's leading citizens. He chose a site on Columbus Avenue in the city and had erected a lavish home, complete with ballroom and indoor water fountain. The mansion was to be his winter residence and soon became the hub of Sandusky's social life during the colder months. Boeckling spent his summers at Cedar Point in a more modest, but nonetheless interesting, octagon house he had built near the lakeshore.

From its humble beginnings as a beer garden in 1870, Cedar Point had evolved into a multi-million dollar playground; and from his equally humble start, George A. Boeckling had become a millionaire. The war years of 1917-18 would cause many frustrations at the resort, but Cedar Point and its president entered the postwar "prosperity" years at full stride.

The splendid Breakers Hotel, which opened its doors in 1905, became one of the largest resort hotels in the Midwest.

Mrs. and Mrs. Eugene Hipp Collection

The east wing of the Breakers Hotel, showing the elevated walkway that led to a sundeck overlooking the beach.

Hayes Presidential Center/Frohman Collection

The elaborate Japanese writing room in the Breakers Hotel.

Hayes Presidential Center/Frohman Collection

By about 1910, the Japanese writing room had been refurnished in more serviceable wicker.

Hayes Presidential Center/Frohman Collection

The hallways of the Breakers were bright and breezy.
Hayes Presidential Center/Frohman Collection

The wooden walkway that led past the vaudeville theatre to the Breakers was later replaced with a covered concrete walk.
Hayes Presidential Center/
Frohman Collection

The massive Coliseum offered a rathskeller on its main floor and a dancing area above.

Hayes Presidential Center/Frohman Collection

The sleek steamer *Eastland* initiated Cleveland-to-Cedar Point service in 1907, and maintained the route through the 1913 season.

Great Lakes Historical Society

Lagoon boats carried steamship passengers from the lake pier near the tip of the peninsula to the center of the resort.

Hayes Presidential Center/Frohman Collection

The new Amusement Circle, 1906.

Hayes Presidential Center/ Frohman Collection

The new powerhouse permitted a colorful illumination of the Amusement Circle.

Mr. and Mrs. Eugene Hipp Collection

Fred Ingersoll's circle swing, located between the Coliseum and the midway buildings, was the centerpiece of the Amusement Circle.

Cedar Point Archives

Built in 1909, the beloved *G. A. Boeckling* served on the Sandusky-to-Cedar Point route for more than forty seasons.

Great Lakes Historical Society

Glenn Curtiss and his Albany Flyer on the Cedar Point beach, 1910.

Mr. and Mrs. Eugene Hipp Collection

A flying boat on the beach about 1914.

George A. Boeckling Collection

Animal shows were always hits at Cedar Point. Here, about 1910, a group of performers stroll along the boardwalk.

Mr. and Mrs. Eugene Hipp Collection

The new bathhouse of 1910 was declared the largest in the world.

Hayes Presidential Center/Frohman Collection

By 1905, Cedar Point employed so many summer workers that dormitories were built behind the Breakers.

Norman Burns Collection

The new Administration Building.
Cedar Point Archives

The Postal Shop near the Administration Building sold thousands of colored postcards each season.
Cedar Point Archives

In 1907, the Cedar Point Post Office was housed in a tiny structure . . . later it was moved to a pagoda near the Coliseum.

Follett House Collection

Resort employees prepare for a boat ride on the lagoons about 1910.

Pat Gerstner Collection

The Okoboji Indians held trapshooting contests at Cedar Point every June.

Mr. and Mrs. Eugene Hipp Collection

The Cedars Hotel, which opened in 1915.

Alden Photographers, Sandusky

By 1915, the prosperous G. A. Boeckling could find a few minutes to frolic in the photo gallery.

George A. Boeckling Collection

On a busy afternoon, the *A. Wehrle, Jr.* and the *G. A. Boeckling* pass on Sandusky Bay.

Hayes Presidential Center/Frohman Collection

With a capacity crowd of 2,500, the *Eastland* prepares to leave Cleveland for Cedar Point on July 4, 1909. Captain M. S. Thompson stands on the docking bridge.

During the late spring of 1910, a large crew of carpenters and painters were hurrying to complete the new bath house for the June opening.

Hayes Presidential Center/Frohman Collection

Legendary football coach Knute Rockne (second from the right), was part of the beach patrol in 1913.

Cedar Point Archives

A steam engine and Brush dynamos in the new powerhouse helped meet the electrical demands of the new midway in 1906.

Hayes Presidential Center/Frohman Collection

A live burrow and a Civil War revolver were some of the props available at J. F. Short's photo studio around 1910.

Authors' Collection

Three well-dressed visitors on the "Lover's Bridge" in the picnic grove.

Author's Collection

In 1908, summer cottages were crude and lacked electricity. Nevertheless, a season's rental cost only $150.00.

Laura M. Stellhorn Collection

Passengers from Cleveland stream toward the resort area after arriving on the *State of Ohio*.

Authors' Collection

The crew of winter caretakers, who patrolled the resort and kept the power house operating, relax in the living room of the Hermitage in 1910. George Boeckling's brother, Gus, is seated third from the left.

Mary Biechele Collection

The steamer *State of Ohio* began service from Toledo in 1908 and was placed on the Cleveland-Cedar Point run in 1914.

Great Lakes Historical Society

The magnificent new bath house with the domes of The Coliseum visible in the background.

Cedar Point Archives

The entrance to the miniature steam railway, with a sign that promised a view of "The Jungles" of Cedar Point.

Cedar Point Archives

Interior of the Igorrote Village, 1907.

Cedar Point Archives

The view from the front seat of the Scenic Railway, about 1910.

Chapter Six

The Resort During the 1920s

By the time World War I came to an end, Cedar Point was a mature resort at the pinnacle of its development. Of course, some expansion did take place during the 1920s, but the resort's major physical plant was fully established by 1920. The two giant hotels, the Coliseum, the Amusement Circle, the lagoons and many other buildings and attractions had all been constructed during the decade preceding the war.

Cedar Point, like almost all amusement parks and resorts, enjoyed great prosperity during the 1920s, but the era of building gigantic hotels and funding expensive expansion projects had come to an end. There were many reasons for this, but among the most important was the fact that Cedar Point was already a huge and profitable operation with sprawling facilities in excellent condition. With so much to offer already, there was certainly some question as to the need for further expansion.

Another factor was Boeckling himself. Since he turned sixty years of age in 1922, it may be that his aggressive spirit was slowing down. But more importantly, he privately suspected that the prosperity of the 1920s would not last, and he also became mildly pessimistic about the resort's future under the new laws of Prohibition. Liquor and beer sales had been a major foundation upon which Cedar Point was built, and without bar revenues, it was not clear how the character of the resort might be altered.

Also, there were external forces that were changing not only Cedar Point, but the entire summer resort industry. Because automobile ownership was now within reach of most families, one-day trips to resorts were becoming more common and long stays at summer hotels were becoming less common. By the late 1920s, the hotel business was not the thriving operation that it had been in 1916, although the booking of major conventions still helped maintain a brisk hotel trade. But if the hotel business was starting to wane, the families that came by automobile for one-day outings

brought more patronage to the amusement area, and during the 1920s this section of the resort took on greater importance.

The resort's entertainment bill also experienced some major upheavals during the 1920s. Vaudeville, a show business staple since the 1890s, was rapidly dying; and there was little, except perhaps dancing, to replace the stage shows. Similarly, the great touring concert bands of Sousa and others, who had enjoyed immense popularity for three decades, were now being replaced by small jazz bands, dance bands, and the novelty of radio, talking movies and the improved phonograph. So, as Cedar Point entered the 1920s, it was forced to cater to a different type of clientele, to discontinue old forms of entertainment, and to appeal to changing public tastes.

The biggest adjustment that Cedar Point had to make was to face the fact that Prohibition had become law, and on July 1, 1919, alcoholic beverages would disappear from the resort for the first time in fifty years. Although publicly Boeckling claimed that Prohibition would not affect the resort, and that, in fact, liquor sales had been declining for a number of years, there is no question that Cedar Point had lost a primary source of income. The most immediate problem, however, was converting the resort's large bars and taverns into legal refreshment operations. The Crystal Rock Castle, long known as a retreat for "lovers of Bohemian life," was converted to Ye Old Castle Grill, a quality restaurant serving steaks, chops and seafoods late into the evening. In the Breakers lobby, a soft drink parlor was installed; and in the Rathskeller, the massive beer hall on the main floor of the Coliseum, a lunchroom and soft drink parlor were separated by attractive latticework. Everywhere beer, liquor and wine had once flowed, sandwiches, soft drinks and ice cream now dominated. As the season progressed, Boeckling's concerns faded, and 1919 proved an excellent year even without the benefit of beer sales. But replacing thousands of dollars in liquor sales was not an easy task; and by July, Boeckling confided to a relative that "...this has been the hardest season I have ever put in at Cedar Point; it keeps me on the go all the time."

Although liquor could not be legally sold at Cedar Point, it was a well-known fact that important guests and the friends of management could always find a drink at the resort. Boeckling had many friends, but because he was a wealthy man with much influence, he also had his share of enemies. One of these foes anonymously suggested to Prohibition agents that quantities of illegal liquor were stored at the resort. Simultaneously, agents raided the resort, the Boeckling mansion, and the homes of resort officers, August Kuebeler, Jr., William Dehnel and Alex M. Wagner. At the resort's Administration Building the agents uncovered a barrel of gin, cases of liquor and champagne, and miscellaneous bottles. When resort employees resisted the search, arrests were made and charges were filed against Boeckling and the others. Although Kuebeler, Dehnel and Wagner were fined, Boeckling was acquitted after convincing the court that his liquor was leftover from before Prohibition. In all probability, liquor continued to be secretly available to selected people at Cedar Point throughout the 1920s, and rumors often circulated that Boeckling was personally involved in rum running. Although no proof of such involvement ever surfaced, gossip contended that fast speedboats carrying contraband eluded the Coast Guard and entered the maze of the lagoons to land their cargoes at the resort.

Primarily because of the automobile, transportation trends at the resort were also slowly changing. The fact that the old wooden dock was replaced in 1923 with a new covered concrete pier suggests that the steamer *Boeckling* was still busy, but she seldom required the assistance of chartered steamers, as had been common during the pre-war years. The steamers from Cleveland, Detroit and Toledo were also still patronized. A ticket from Cleveland on the *Goodtime* still cost less than two dollars, and convention visitors could travel all the way from Buffalo for less than six dollars. At the resort, transporting the in-bound passengers from the pier to the resort was made more convenient in 1924, when a concrete roadway was constructed. The old 1911 lagoon boats were still available, but on the new roadway gasoline-powered trams designed by Lester Sears, the founder of Towmotor Corporation, operated whenever steamers were at the docks. These trams were employed until steamer service ended after World War II.

The railroads continued to schedule large excursions, but patronage of the electric railways declined drastically during the 1920s. By 1927, the future of the Lake Shore Electric was in question; and two years earlier, the Toledo, Port Clinton & Lakeside aban-

doned its Bay Shore extension which had been connected to Cedar Point by a small boat line since 1912. With 20,000,000 automobiles registered in the United States by 1925, it was clear that gradually the automobile was replacing the steamship and the rail lines. At Cedar Point, the presence of the car was increasingly apparent, and on July 3, 1921, 3,000 automobiles were counted in the resort's parking lots. As early as 1917, Boeckling had started to plan for parking garages, and in 1924, a huge steel garage capable of holding 500 cars was built inside the structure of The Racer roller coaster. He also installed two gasoline stations, one at the new garages and another at the entrance road.

As the number of cars visiting the resort increased, major traffic jams on the entrance road became common during the 1920s. To help eliminate these delays, as well as to accommodate larger numbers of cars, Boeckling began to plan for a bridge that would connect the peninsula with the mainland. In 1926, a New York firm completed a study for a proposed bridge linking Cedar Point with both Sandusky and Marblehead, but the estimated cost of $2,500,000 made the project impractical. However, in 1928, Boeckling envisioned a bridge from the mainland to a spot on the peninsula near Biemiller's Cove. A year later, the Cedar Point Bridge Company was formed, and legislation allowing the bridge's construction was passed by Sandusky, the State of Ohio and the United States Congress. By the time all of this legislation had been passed, however, the stock market disaster of October, 1929 had occurred, and Boeckling wisely postponed the bridge project. The bridge company, however, was never dissolved, and twenty years after Boeckling's death a bridge which greatly reduced travel time to the resort became a reality.

At least until the mid-1920s, hotel business at Cedar Point remained very good. In fact, on many weekends, the reservation clerks received twice as many requests for rooms as they could accommodate. In 1919, Boeckling proposed the construction of a massive 2,000-room hotel to the north of the Breakers. Such a structure, had it been built, would have been only slightly smaller than the world's largest hotel, New York's Hotel Pennsylvania. In 1921, he further announced that plans for a year-round Spanish-style hotel in the residential section were still alive; and a year later, he even thought about becoming a partner in a new 350-room hotel at Put-in-Bay. None of these ambitious plans advanced beyond the stage of architectural consultation, however. Perhaps Boeckling now realized that the era of the great summer hotel was coming to an end. He may have watched New York's Coney Island, where the transformation to a working-class resort had brought about the closings of the once great Manhattan Beach, Brighton Beach, Oriental and

Sea Beach Palace hotels. Whatever his reasons may have been, Boeckling was content to add another 160-room wing, called the Bon Air section, to the Breakers. The opening of the Bon Air addition in 1926 gave the Breakers a grand total of 875 rooms and the entire resort a total of more than 1,100 rooms. At about the same time, a Western Union Telegraph office was opened in the Breakers. This service facilitated faster reservations and also permitted vacationing businessmen to maintain contact with the financial world.

Throughout the 1920s, resort guests were treated to dining room cuisine which rivaled that of the best cosmopolitan hotels. The dining room was located in the northeastern corner of the Grand Pavilion, where screened windows admitted lake breezes and ceiling fans provided pleasant dining on even the warmest afternoons. The dining room staff included conservatively attired hostesses and two hundred college girls in spotless white waitress uniforms. And, during the evening supper hour, a small ensemble provided soft background music for the enjoyment of the diners.

In 1927, Boeckling hired as his new head chef, Henri Rigo, the well-known chef from Cleveland's Hollenden House Hotel. Under Rigo's direction, the cuisine at Cedar Point became legendary. A typical luncheon menu might include clam chowder, seafood cocktail, fillet of sole, sweetbread croquettes, roast short ribs, Spring Chicken Maryland, and an assortment of steaks and chops. The desserts, of course, were served fresh daily from Cedar Point's own ovens. The demanding Boeckling kept constant watch on the dining room, and was, himself, a regular patron, occupying the same table each evening at eight o'clock. Not only did the dining room and the nearby cafeteria serve the finest meals, they also served them in great numbers. Over the two-day July 4th holiday of 1927, for example, the dining room alone served 10,000 meals.

As the decade wore on, a definite shift in the resort's patronage became apparent. While, in the past, the majority of guests had stayed for one or more nights at the Point, they now came by car for short one-day visits. Because their time at Cedar Point was limited, packing the most fun into each hour became essential. As a result, the Amusement Circle took on added importance, and predictably, modernization and expansion of the circle followed. New, innovative amusement rides began appearing at Cedar Point, and many of the older attractions from the 1906 midway disappeared. The original auto ride, Ingersoll's massive circle swing, The Racer coaster, A Trip to Rockaway, and many other rides and shows were replaced with more modern ones. At the same time, many of the early concessionaires entered into partnerships and created companies, each of which operated several midway attractions. In 1925, Roy Parker, David Steinemann and J. B. Sutton combined their concessions to form the Concourse Amusement Company. In so doing, they became the largest ride operator at Cedar Point and were responsible for most of the new ride installations of the 1920s. Two years later, Tony Anast, Leo Finkler and George Stinson amalgamated their numerous game concessions and frozen custard stands to become the largest games operator at the resort. Most of these concessionaires were self-made businessmen who had started working at the resort as teenagers and had gradually acquired concessions. Finkler had begun his career as a pier employee in 1915, and Anast had worked his way from "smashing" baggage to hotel bellhop and then to Coliseum waiter in 1918. By the late 1920s, all were prosperous midway concession operators.

The primary attractions of the Amusement Circle were, of course, the mechanical amusement rides. Most rides were designed for adults, but in 1924, a kiddieland made up of miniaturized rides for young children was installed. A year later, the Concourse Amusement Company built a unique concept in fun houses called Noah's Ark. Originally developed in 1919, Noah's Ark featured a large boat resting on top of a replica of Mt. Ararat. From windows on the Ark's deck, the heads of wooden animals greeted the customer who entered the hull to be entertained by a variety of fun house stunts, including floors that moved. Deep inside the structure of Noah's Ark, and unseen by the crowds, was the office of Roy Parker, a retreat where, on quiet days, a group of concessionaires gathered for friendly card games.

By 1927, the business on the midway was so good that concessionaires added a Shoot-the-Chutes water ride, the newly invented Tilt-A-Whirl, and a colorful walk-through called Bluebeard's Palace. Developed by Frank Thomas, the latter had been successfully installed in six other parks by 1927. Themed around the adventures of Bluebeard the pirate, funseekers were treated to moving floors, air jets, revolving barrels and even mild electric shocks.

The most exciting addition to the midway, however, was the magnificent Cyclone roller coaster, a ride that boasted the slogan "Scientifically Built for Speed." In 1929, the Cedar Point Coaster Company, another Boeckling subsidiary, hired noted coaster builder Harry Traver to install the most thrilling coaster ever opened at the resort. Using plans prepared by Fred Church of Venice, California, Traver created an awesome, bone-jarring coaster on the site of the recently razed Racer. Not as large as Traver's horrifying coasters at Crystal Beach, Palisades Park, or Revere Beach, the Cedar Point Cyclone was, nonetheless, one of the finest coasters ever constructed in the midwest. Steep hills, sharply-banked turns and spiralling descents soon made the Cyclone a legend.

Almost in the shadow of the Cyclone, many of the older rides continued to flourish. The Finley Family, operators of a West Virginia lumber yard, had continued success with the Leap Frog Railway, as did the T.M. Harton Company with their Leap the Dips. Neither coaster was equal to the Cyclone, but both prospered throughout the 1920s. Even Harton's carousel thrived, grossing over $3,500 in 1922. While this may seem like a small income for an entire summer of operation, consider the fact that a year's insurance for the ride was less than sixteen dollars, and fifteen dollars bought enough rolls of tickets to last several seasons. Other successful rides of the 1920s included S.W. Potter's Custer Cars, Charley Daley's Sea Swings, Heine Gross' miniature steamtrain and, until removed to make room for the Cyclone, Joe Ottinger's Racer.

Along the boardwalk, in the bathhouse, in the Concourse building, and throughout the midway were dozens of games of chance. Most games were wheels of fortune, which offered such prizes as plush elephants and dogs, silk shirts, dolls, parasols, fruit and cigarettes. One game, Tony Anast's Ukulele Wheel, took advantage of a major 1920s fad and gave away more than 100,000 of the small, stringed instruments during the decade. Other games included fish ponds, guess-your-weight scales, hi-strikers, cat racks, Japanese string games and an electric monkey race track. The Monkey Race featured live monkeys that sat in little electric race cars that were controlled by the players. The player operating the winning car received a blanket. And for those who were not successful at one of the games but wanted to carry home a souvenir, George McClain ran a small stand in front of the Old Mill where he handpainted and lettered glassware. Other midway attractions during these seasons included a wild animal circus, Whippet racing and a host of lesser operations.

On the beach, airplane rides continued their popularity; and in 1920, the resort hired Alfred Flazell, an English aviator who had recently been a hit in Atlantic City. But the beach was also used for less thrilling events, including a large outdoor checkers tournament that was started in 1924. Floodlights were installed on the beach during these years in the hope that night bathing would catch on. The idea was a failure despite the fact that night bathing had been a popular pastime on the peninsula for years, sometimes without the formality of bathing suits. In fact, in 1922, five people were arrested by the Cedar Point police for nude bathing near the residential section.

Just as Cedar Point had been a pioneer in the exhibition of early motion pictures, it was also one of the first locations in the world to publicly present "talking pictures." A sound movie produced with early

Western Electric equipment was shown at the 1926 Ohio Telephone Convention held at Cedar Point. Only four times before had a "talkie" been seen anywhere in the world. The exhibition at Cedar Point preceded Warner Brothers' *The Jazz Singer* (often touted as the first talking picture) by more than a year; and it would be two years later that Sandusky's State Theatre offered its patrons their first sound movie.

During the 1920s, Cedar Point's management became even more aggressive in soliciting regional and national conventions. The culmination of these efforts came in 1925, when the Lions Club selected the resort for their national convention. Not only did this convention attract one of the largest crowds in the resort's history, but it also became a landmark convention for the Lions. Invited to address the assembly was Helen Keller, who challenged the 7,500 Lions in the audience to establish a commitment to help prevent blindness and promote healthy eye care. Her moving speech in 1925 proved to be the impetus for what has become a world-wide crusade for saving sight.

The 1920s also witnessed the first attempt to book special events that extended the resort's season beyond Labor Day. For several seasons the Coliseum's dance floor was kept open throughout September, and in both 1919 and 1922, portions of the resort were opened after Labor Day to accommodate the huge convention of Pastor Russell's International Bible Students' Association. Attracting over 10,000 students, these conventions filled both Cedar Point hotels and required thousands of the conventioneers to stay in Sandusky hotels. A unique aspect of Pastor Russell's conventions at Cedar Point were the mass baptisms that took place in the shallow water off the bathing beach.

Because resorts and amusement parks were built almost totally of wood, fires and other natural disasters routinely destroyed buildings and entire parks. At Coney Island, in 1911, a major fire razed Dreamland Park in its entirety, and along the East Coast, hurricanes were known to topple roller coasters and wash piers into the sea. But Cedar Point had been spared most catastrophies and, in fact, its Model T firetruck saw so little use that it fell into disrepair and often rested on flat tires. The resort's closest brush with a natural disaster came on June 28, 1924, when severe thunderstorms and a vicious tornado passed directly over the peninsula, smashing into Sandusky and Lorain with deadly force. Damage to the resort was minor, but stories in newspapers from as far away as the East Coast claimed that Cedar Point had been all but destroyed. However, the high winds did produce major damage at the resort's Sandusky pier, sinking the launch *Columbus* and demolishing the passenger terminal. Fortunately, the steamer *Boeckling* was just preparing to leave Cedar Point at the time of the storm or she, too, might have been a victim. For several years, Boeckling had been considering the construction of a winter office building in Sandusky. The destruction of the passenger terminal provided an opportunity to move the ferry operations to the west side of the slip, build a new passenger shelter, and include an attractive off-season administration building in the plans. For the next thirty years, the resort's winter offices were maintained at the south end of the ferry dock in Sandusky.

The economic boom of the 1920s brought to Cedar Point, and to most resorts, a high level of prosperity. The 1920 season was, claimed Boeckling, the greatest year in the resort's history and a full thirty percent ahead of 1919 in gross revenues. By 1924, the G. A. Boeckling Company had an income of over $1,000,000, and this figure did not include the income of dozens of concessionaires. Even when a season was plagued with rain, as was 1926, Boeckling was able to declare stock dividends of $37,500. The value of the property owned by the Boeckling Company was set at almost $3,000,000 by tax appraisers in 1926, although, through five years of litigation, Boeckling eventually forced a reappraisal to less than $1,000,000. In an era when a quart of milk cost fifteen cents and many working men earned salaries of only thirty-five dollars per week, the value of Boeckling's property and the resort's yearly income were truly impressive.

Cedar Point's success, and that of George Boeckling, ran a parallel course. In 1922, on the occasion of his 25th year in Sandusky, the Sandusky *Register* called him the man who made Cedar Point and stated: "Mr. Boeckling, by his accomplishments, has achieved a reputation as one of the country's half-dozen great directors of public amusements and recreation." At this time, he was at the pinnacle of power and respect. A local bank, the Third National, elected him president, and in Cleveland he was admitted to the prestigious Union Club. He owned stock in many local companies, and the Sandusky Chamber of Commerce selected him as their president. Yet, he was first and foremost a showman, and during his tenure as president of the Third National Bank, he often carried in his pocket a sheet of uncut and unsigned currency. When making a purchase, he would produce the sheet of currency with a flourish and, with the scissors he also carried, snip off the required number of bills, which he then signed as bank president, to the astonishment of merchant, shopkeeper and restauranteur alike. While the practice was tolerated with some amusement in Sandusky, it no doubt caused him many unnecessary problems when traveling. But, that was George Arthur Boeckling: master showman, supreme egotist.

SCENIC RAILWAY
ABOUT 1920

George A. Boeckling in 1922 . . . on the occasion of his sixtieth birthday and twenty-fifth year at Cedar Point.

George A. Boeckling Collection

The Leap Frog scenic railway during the 1920s.

Hayes Presidential Center/
Frohman Collection

The C & B Line bought the *Goodtime* exclusively to handle the big crowds on the Cleveland-to-Cedar Point and Put-in-Bay route.

Great Lakes Historical Society

In 1924, a concrete road was built from the lake pier to the center of the resort and trams were purchased to transport steamship passengers.

Follett House Collection

Bill Stinson's Monkey Ball Game in 1922.

Albert Fresch Collection

The Leap the Dips coaster's second hill.

In 1919 and 1922, the International Bible Students' Association held mass baptisms on the beach.

Hayes Presidential Center/
Frohman Collection

In 1926, the *City of Toledo* operated from Detroit to Cedar Point and Sandusky.

Great Lakes Historical Society

The dining room during the 1920s.

Albert Fresch Collection

Stinson's Waffle Stand, 1925.

Albert Fresch Collection

The lift hill of the Leap the Dips coaster.

Hayes Presidential Center/
Frohman Collection

Noah's Ark, a unique funhouse
built in 1925 for the Concourse
Amusement Company.

Hayes Presidential Center/
Frohman Collection

The beach and the boardwalk, 1927.

Norman Burns Collection

A typical Cedar Point midway game of the 1920s.
Hayes Presidential Center/
Frohman Collection

An aerial view of the resort section, 1929. The roller coasters are (left to right) the new Cyclone, the Leap Frog and the Leap the Dips.

Cedar Point Archives

By 1920, Cedar Point's advertising effort included billboards that appeared in Cleveland, Toledo, Detroit and other cities.

Cedar Point Archives

The resort's famous dining room required a staff of twenty chefs, dozens of waitresses and numerous other employees. During the two-day July 4th holiday of 1927, this crew served more than 10,000 meals.

Cedar Point Archives

Meredith Price's Orchestra provided afternoon and evening dance music in 1927.

Raymond Roop Collection

Throughout the 1920s, the hotel business was so good that the barber shop at Hotel Breakers required a staff of twelve barbers.

George A. Boeckling Collection

A service railroad connected the bay pier with the warehouses and other buildings that received supplies and baggage. Originally horse-powered, the railroad was converted to steam power and, later, to a gasoline locomotive.

Authors' Collection

By 1925, Hotel Breakers was twenty years old and much of the building's facade was covered with ivy. In addition, shade trees had grown tall around the hotel.　　Cedar Point Archives

The Bon Air addition to Hotel Breakers, completed in 1926, was the final hotel expansion for the Boeckling era.

Cedar Point Archives

A postcard view of the Cedars Hotel during the 1920s. In the foreground are some of the rowboats that were available for rental.

Authors' Collection

The Water Toboggan was still a popular fixture on the beach in 1925.

Authors' Collection

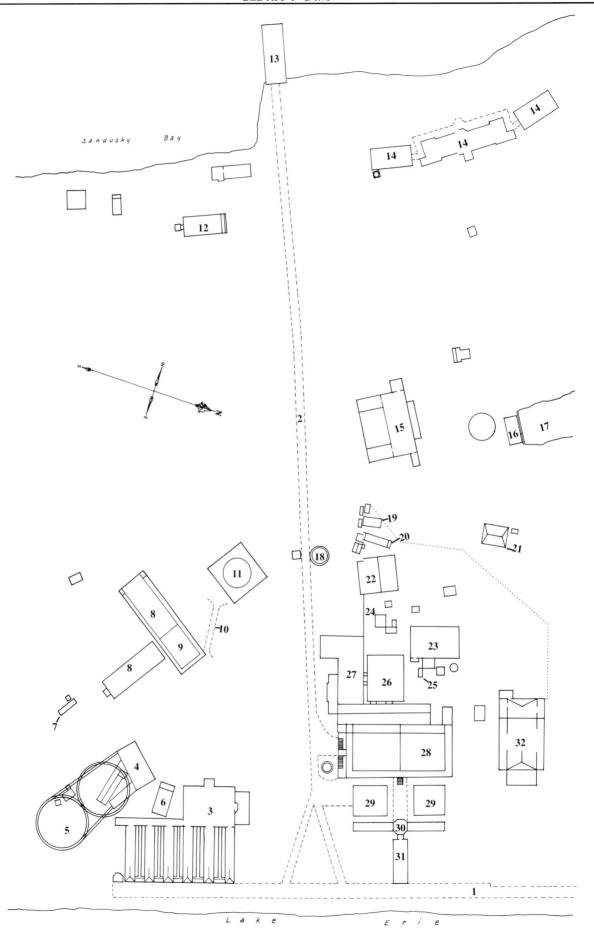

Map of Cedar Point - 1905

1. Boardwalk
2. Walkway from Pier to Boardwalk
3. Bath House
4. Racer Roller Coaster
5. Hotel Breakers
6. Laughing Gallery
7. Miniature Railway Station
8. Bowling Alleys
9. Moving Picture Theater / Rathskeller
10. Lover's Bridge
11. Carrousel
12. Bay Shore Hotel
13. Pier
14. White House Hotel
15. Crystal Rock Castle
16. Canoe/Boat Landing
17. Lagoons
18. Candy Stand
19. Photo Studio
20. Shooting Gallery
21. Pumping Station
22. Powerhouse
23. Ice House
24. Laundry
25. Ice Cream Plant
26. Kitchen
27. Dining Room
28. Grand Pavilion
29. Refreshment Pavilions
30. Band Stand
31. Penny Arcade
32. Vaudeville Theater

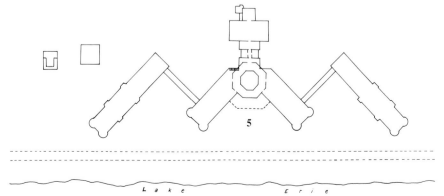

Map of Cedar Point Amusement Area - 1935

1   Bathhouse
2.   Small Merry-Go-Round
3.   Ferris Wheel
4.   Joy Plane
5.   Cyclone Roller Coaster
6.   Automobile Parking Garages
7.   Rest Rooms
8.   Candy Stand
9.   Photo Studio
10.   Tumble Inn (Funhouse)
11.   The Orange Mill
12.   Dark Ride Cold Cascades Building
13.   High Frolics Roller Coaster
14.   "Old" Concourse (Games & Food)
15.   The Coliseum
16.   Seaplane
17.   Venetian Swings
18.   "New" Concourse
19.   Tumble Bug
20.   Octopus
21.   Miniature Railway Station
22.   Oriental Dancers
23.   Caterpillar
24.   Pony Track
25.   Midget Autos
26.   Auto Skooter
27.   Carousel
28.   Leaping Lena
29.   Noah's Ark
30.   Hilarity Hall (Funhouse)
31.   Leap the Dips Roller Coaster
32.   Edan Musee (Wax Museum)
33.   Blue Beard's Palace
34.   Pier
35.   Dormitory
36.   Coffee Stand

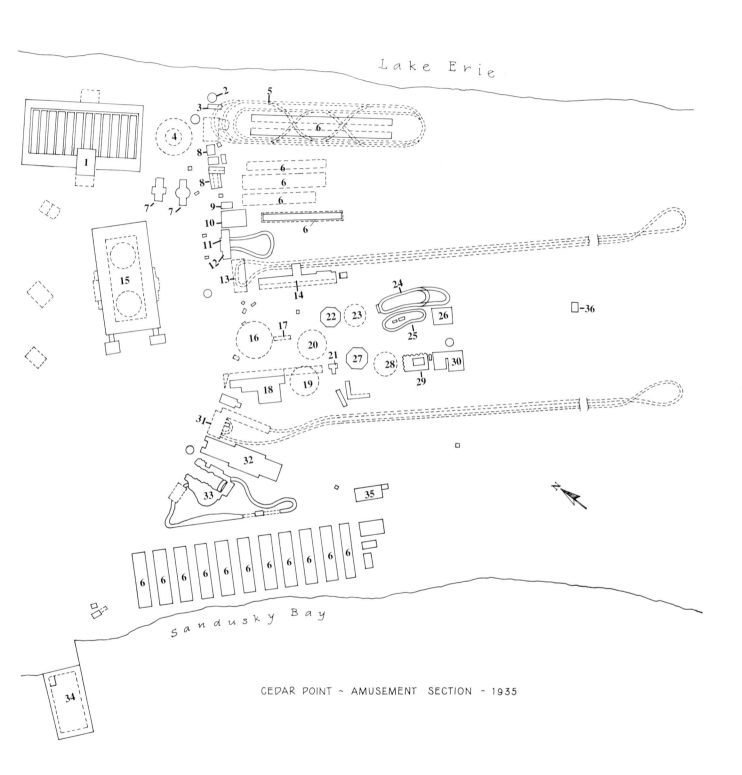

Lake Erie

Sandusky Bay

CEDAR POINT ~ AMUSEMENT SECTION ~ 1935

By 1929, the Amusement Circle was dominated by three large roller coasters. From top to bottom are the Cyclone, the Leap Frog Railway (renamed High Frolics in 1934), and the Leap the Dips. Cedar Point Archives

In 1929, Cedar Point was still heavily tree covered and most of the northern tip was undeveloped. Most of the roads and the amusement area were unpaved. Cedar Point Archives

Chapter Seven

Depression and War

When Cedar Point opened for the 1929 season on a rainy Saturday morning, George Boeckling was seriously ill and confined to his Sandusky home. A year earlier a Sandusky doctor had informed Boeckling that he was suffering from chronic nephritis, and as this condition worsened, he became less able to oversee Cedar Point's operations. In his absence, trusted lieutenants Edward A. Smith, August Kuebeler, Jr., and Joseph Singler ran the resort. Boeckling spent a number of weeks in a Cleveland hospital, and on several occasions he neared death, only to rally once more. As rumors of Boeckling's illness spread many feared that the end of Cedar Point as a great resort was near. The State of Ohio, which was searching for a site for a penal colony to house 500 of the State's worst criminals, considered buying Cedar Point. Because of Boeckling's condition, the State believed that the $6,000,000 property could be obtained for a fraction of its real value.

By 1931, Boeckling was confined to a wheelchair, but his devotion to Cedar Point and his iron will compelled him to make attempts to visit the resort. Believing that Cedar Point could not be properly operated without his personal supervision, Boeckling arranged to be wheeled around the grounds by an employee or a relative. On July 4th, he enhanced the fatherly image that he had acquired among the employees by distributing dollar bills to his legion of workers. Soon after, the effects of the summer heat and Boeckling's worsening physical condition caused a complete collapse. Taken to his home, he developed uremia and died at 5 P.M. on July 24, 1931.

The funeral that followed Boeckling's death was befitting a showman. On the night before the funeral, the Sandusky Boys' and Girls' Band, which he had long supported, visited his home. At the time of the funeral procession, his photograph in the Breakers Hotel was draped in black crepe, flags at the resort and on the steamer that bore his name dipped to half mast and at the powerhouse the steam whistle sounded

a long salute. Over his grave at Oakwood Cemetary, a $6,000 peristyle marks the final resting place of a great businessman and exceptional promoter. Boeckling himself could not have devised a more fitting end to his rather spectacular life.

While a Sandusky newspaper editor had once described Boeckling as an overbearing egotist, a local attorney described him as "...a man of practical dreams with the genius and initiative to carry them into actualities." It was precisely this practical business nature which prompted Boeckling to plan for the perpetuation of Cedar Point by establishing a trust fund, with a major Cleveland bank as administrator. At the time of his death, Boeckling's stock in the G. A. Boeckling Company was worth as much as $750,000, and much of this stock became the nucleus of the trust. The profits of the trust were intended to help support deserving educational, recreational and charitable projects. Such philanthropy was not unusual for Boeckling who had, in the late 1920s, donated $25,000 to Sandusky's Providence Hospital and a large pipe organ to St. Mary's Church. Considering Cedar Point's flourishing business in the 1920s, both Boeckling and the trust officers had reason to believe that his trust would produce large charitable funds. What they could not anticipate, of course, was the economic collapse of the 1930s.

Although over 1,000,000 people visited Cedar Point in 1930, and the company reported gross revenues in excess of $1,000,000, the effects of a deepening national depression were becoming obvious. All around the country, amusement parks and summer resorts were starting to suffer. By the end of the 1930 season, seventy-two percent of the nation's amusement parks reported declining revenues, some by as much as thirty-five percent. A year later, eighty-five percent admitted that poor business conditons had cut deeply into profits. In a single season, Cincinnati's well-managed Coney Island watched its attendance figures drop by thirteen percent. Picnic bookings and conventions, the heart of Cedar Point's trade, saw a forty-one percent decline between 1929 and 1930. Little did park and resort operators realize that worse conditions were to arrive before the mid-1930s.

The death of George Boeckling created a vacancy that was difficult to fill, especially in the midst of a worsening economic environment. Immediately after Boeckling's death, Alex M. Wagner, a local banker and brother-in-law of the late entrepreneur, became president of the resort company. Due to other business obligations, however, Wagner agreeably resigned to allow George's brother, A. R. Boeckling, to assume the office. Many hoped that by returning the magical Boeckling name to the resort, Cedar Point would be able to reverse its declining business trend. But the new president had many of his own business concerns in Indiana to occupy his time. A few years later, A. R. Boeckling died, and Ed Smith was elected president. Smith and the company's vice president, August Kuebeler, Jr., were able and experienced managers, but they chose to operate Cedar Point along old and familiar lines at a time when only innovation would keep the resort profitable. In addition, Smith and Kuebeler were often restrained by the cautious trust officers who were usually unwilling to invest in improvements.

Any attempt to operate Cedar Point within the business practices of the 1920s was doomed to failure, for both society and economics had changed drastically in just a few years. Vaudeville, once the core of the resort's entertainment fare, was extinct; and throughout the nation, vaudeville theatres were either razed or became motion picture houses. Concert bands, too, were all but totally gone. Dancing was still a popular pastime, but the wave of popularity generated by the Big Bands did not arrive until the late 1930s.

Methods of transportation were also greatly altered during the depression years. Automobiles were numerous, but few could afford to waste gasoline on a trip to a summer resort. Railroads could no longer maintain excursion services, and gradually the passenger trains that had once filled the tracks along Sandusky's waterfront dissappeared. Interurban railways throughout the country went bankrupt, and all but a few ceased operations. The Lakeshore Electric, which annually brought thousands to Cedar Point from Cleveland and Toledo, abandoned its last passenger service just before the opening of the 1938 season. Only the steamship service from Cleveland, Detroit and Toledo remained, and even those routes were often in jeopardy throughout the 1930s. Every factor of the economy seemed to be conspiring against Cedar Point.

The G. A. Boeckling Company reported its last profit in 1931, and for the next twenty years it would be unable to pay its shareholders even modest dividends.

But, if the Boeckling Company and its shareholders suffered, the effects of the Depression on the concessionaires who owned rides, games and food stands was even more devastating. These were the people who annually paid the resort a rental fee for a small building in the midway area. Most of the concessionaires from outside the Sandusky area either rented a room at one of the hotels or lived in cramped rooms behind their concessions. Some, like the gypsy fortune tellers, spent the summer at the campgrounds near the bay dock. Most of the concessionaires barely eked out a living during the Depression, depending on the larger weekend and holiday crowds for their livelihood. In fact, on weekdays the midway often closed after the Cleveland and Detroit boats departed in the late afternoon and did not reopen until the next day. Although none of the concessionaires made much money, the Depression seems to have had a different effect on each operation. For Tony Anast, the fact that customers had less money greatly reduced his game income but stimulated business at his Concourse restaurant where breakfast prices were lower than in the resort's main dining room. On the other hand, Frederick Posner had the misfortune to arrive at the resort in the depth of the Depression. In 1932, Posner took over the Crystal Rock Castle and converted it to the Castle Sandwich Shop, where he specialized in hot corned beef sandwiches and often remained open around the clock. At the end of the season, Posner tallied his receipts and sadly noted a loss of $500.

Posner did not discourage easily, and despite his losses in 1932, he went on to become a successful concessionaire. Most of the "old timers"—the Stinsons, the Anasts, the Finklers and the Parkers— somehow struggled through the depressed seasons and doggedly refused to close their concessions. Others, however, lost so much money that they left as soon as a season came to an end. Consequently, Ed Smith was constantly advertising for new concessionaires, and as late as April, he was still looking for concessions for the 1933 season. Smith did everything in his power to help the struggling midway concessionaires. When many complained that they were losing money, he lowered their season's rent by as much as fifty percent. Smith's considerate nature also extended to the concessionaires' families. Just before opening day each season, Smith would ride his bicycle from stand to stand leaving a roll of free tickets so that the children could enjoy the midway rides. Thus, in many ways, the management and the concessionaires worked together to ease their beloved Cedar Point through the Depression.

As conditions worsened, the resort's management made every effort to promote the facilities at Cedar Point. In 1932, their advertising strategy centered around the fact that the resort was a good bargain, but with 12,000,000 people out of work nationally, even bargains had little meaning. For the first time in many years, the resort not only permitted fishing on the peninsula, but also rented rowboats and sold bait. In the dining room, full course meals were reduced to one dollar. At the auto entrance on the Chaussee, everyone arriving before 6 p.m. was given five free dance tickets. In the belief that a new appearance might entice larger crowds, a new color scheme was introduced for all the buildings. Instead of the earth tones favored by Boeckling, the buildings were now painted white and green, and over the next few years this new color combination was used on all the major buildings and many of the midway attractions. Even the steamer *Boeckling* eventually had her traditional red trim replaced by green.

None of these innovations had much effect, however, and the economy of Cedar Point, like the nation's, continued to decline. In 1932, many key dates were greeted by either rain or cool weather; and despite estimates of 30,000 people on July 4th and only slightly fewer numbers on Labor Day, the Sandusky *Register* was being charitable when it described 1932 as a "strenuous season."

For the operators of amusement rides on the midway, the declining revenues after 1930, soon presented the problem of how to maintain the rides in top condition on lower budgets. Joseph Finley, whose family operated the Leap Frog scenic railway, soon discovered that his coaster needed a major overhaul. At first, Finley considered avoiding the costs of rebuilding the ride by moving a coaster built in 1928 at Lima to Cedar Point to replace the aging Leap Frog. However, he finally decided to completely rebuild the coaster, and this reconstruction so thoroughly changed the coaster's appearance that it was given a new name: High Frolics. Opening in 1934, High Frolics offered an exciting seventy-four foot first hill (although publicists were constantly claiming that it towered ninety feet above the midway). Even though the track structure had been totally rebuilt, High Frolics still exhibited some of the characteristics of an old scenic railway. The trains were repainted with a fresh coat of green and white, but between the cars there was still a seat for the brakeman who controlled the speed of the trains and engaged the cable that hoisted the cars up the first hill. Many years before, most coaster designers had replaced cables with chains and brakemen with more up-to-date controls. Nevertheless, High Frolics looked like a new coaster and the old favorite enjoyed a new lease on life. Not so fortunate was T.M. Harton's older Leap the Dips coaster, which was also very much in need of major maintenance. However, the Harton Company decided against any further investments, and the ride was abandoned about 1935. It stood unused for a number of seasons until it

was finally razed by a contractor. In the meantime, the Leap the Dips served one final purpose when the train's seat cushions were removed and placed in the High Frolic's cars. For the first time since 1917, Cedar Point was operating only two roller coasters. Fortunately, the daring Cyclone coaster was still quite new and had survived the Depression even though it was somewhat dilapidated by the 1940s.

Unlike the 1920s, there was little expansion of the midway during the 1930s, and except for a Tumble Bug ride installed in 1934, the amusement section changed little. In 1936, the midway included the following:

Kiddie Merry-Go-Round	Venetian Swings
Aero Joy Plane	Ferris Wheel
Scooters	Shoot-the-Rapids
Tumble Bug	Kiddie Kars
Sea Swings	Noah's Ark
Cyclone Coaster	The Eden Musee
Hilarity Hall	Carousel
Caterpillar	Pony Track
High Frolics Coaster	Leaping Lena
The Tumble Inn	Sea Plane
Miniature Railroad	Bluebeard's Palace
Hawaiian Dancing Show	

Among the midway shows and attractions which appeared at Cedar Point during the 1930s were many transients who remained on the peninsula for only one or two seasons. A few of the shows that enjoyed moderate popularity included an exhibit of man-eating tigers from India, a group of Hawaiian hula dancers, and the Austin & Kurtz sideshow that migrated to Cedar Point after an engagement at the Chicago World's Fair. During one season, a new motordrome was built, and Daredevil Dobish and his associates drove midget racers on the "wall of death." The constant turnover of shows and concessions was a good indication of how difficult it was to make a living at Cedar Point during the years of the Great Depression.

The economic woes that plagued the midway concessionaires also extended to the hotels, which had always been the sparkling gems of the resort. Since there were seldom enough guests to even fill one hotel, the Cedars was closed early in the 1930s. Although it was occasionally reopened on holidays or for large conventions, the Cedars was used only as an employee domitory, haunted by the memory of its life during the golden age of resort hotels.

Meanwhile, the Breakers continued to welcome its "regulars" each season. Gus Dorais, the college football coach who, with Rockne, had perfected the forward pass at Cedar Point, was an occasional guest during the 1930s; and members of Hollywood's famous Warner Family took an entire suite of rooms almost every season. But, overall, business at the Breakers was not good, and the hotel struggled to survive throughout the decade. In addition to the basic problems which plagued the resort business during the Depression, the Breakers had not been modernized in any way since its construction in 1905. Then, in 1935, a new manager, H. S. Graves, was hired, and under his direction some important changes began to take place. New private baths and even telephones were added to many rooms, and throughout the hotel, much of the older and most worn furniture was replaced. Arrangements were made to grant hotel guests privileges at the eighteen-hole Plum Brook Country Club golf course on the mainland. Just outside the hotel, new clay tennis courts and a scenic bridle path were added, and after Prohibition ended, the outdoor Terrace Cocktail Lounge was opened. At the Terrace, a stage was built for small dance bands, and tables with colorful umbrellas were spaced throughout the new lounge.

But, perhaps the most interesting addtion to the hotel was the gambling room that managed to survive for a few seasons in what is now the hotel's laundry room. Gambling devices, especially slot machines, were common at Ohio's amusement parks during the 1930s, although their legality was often challenged by local authorities. When Cedar Point's gambling room opened, it was placed under the direction of Charlie McGarvey, a longtime resort manager who had supervised the Coliseum's operation some years earlier. McGarvey's very successful little casino included two craps tables, a dozen slot machines, blackjack tables, and the ever-present roulette wheel. Unfortunately for Cedar Point, Sandusky law enforcement officers forced the casino's closing after just two seasons.

Just when the Depression was reaching its lowest ebb and business conditions were at their gloomiest, the Prohibition laws were repealed. The reinstatement of beer and liquor sales for the 1933 season gave Ed Smith, the directors, and the concessionaires new hope. Quickly, beverage outlets were installed in the Green and Silver Grill, the cafeteria, the Coliseum, the luncheonette, and everywhere else that a cooler or a beer tap could be located. On opening day of 1933, the first glass of beer served in the Coliseum was drawn by Andy Vettel, a young employee whose father had designed and built the Leap the Dips coaster. At Posner's Castle Sandwich Shop, which was open all night, boat-loads of people arrived from Put-in-Bay, where the bars closed at midnight. The Sandusky *Register* reported that "...the Coliseum was crowded with from 3,000 to 4,000 people, dancing, skating, drinking beer and just loafing." The return of beer and liquor seems to have been a turning point for the resort, and on July 4th, the management counted 6,000 cars with license plates from sixteen states and Canada. The attendance that day was estimated at 50,000, and "The Coliseum smacked of old time

crowds with merry makers imbibing refreshments." On the lower floor of the Coliseum, where beer and liquor now flowed, a dance floor was installed, and happy groups of young people danced to the sounds of such bands as Julius Fisher and His Orchestra and Bill Cullitan's Hotel Biltmore Orchestra. Cedar Point's management predicted that beer would return prosperity to the peninsula, and without question, it was one of the factors that helped Cedar Point recover from the darkest days of the 1930s.

One of the first signs of recovery came in 1935, when the volume of mail leaving the resort required the postmaster to increase the substation's staff from one to two clerks. At the end of that season, Ed Smith hired Fred W. Long, a Cleveland advertising executive, to head the resort's newly formed Promotion Department. Within this department, one man concentrated on convention bookings, another on excursions and picnics, while Long dedicated his time to developing much-needed publicity. Under Long's direction, his department became an exhibitor at Cleveland's Great Lakes Exposition of 1936. Here, Long and his associates distributed literature from a booth that featured a backdrop showing the resort's famous boardwalk and beach. Long's other efforts included placing dozens of newspaper stories, entering resort information in travel booklets, distributing thousands of new brochures, and declaring to one and all that Cedar Point was the "Atlantic City of the Middle West." Even the resort's stationery, which had been unchanged for thirty years, was redesigned to reflect the popular art deco styling of the era. Long's efforts were rewarded. The opening day of 1936 was the best in five years; and on July 4th of 1938, he claimed, with some exaggertion, that a crowd of 100,000 had flocked to the resort. By 1939, he could claim, without exaggeration, that both July 4th and Labor Day had been the best holidays of the decade.

It was more than a public relations effort, however, that brought Cedar Point out of the slump of the early 1930s. When other amusement parks reported a revival of the old sport of roller skating, the huge dance floor on the upper level of the Coliseum was easily converted into a gigantic skating rink. The new rink was so outstanding in size that it was selected to host the 1936 Ohio State Roller Skating Championship competition. Attractions which had been favorites at Chicago's Century of Progress in 1933-34, were lured to Cedar Point's midway, and both seaplane rides and parachute exhibitions returned to popularity on the beach. The more sedate pleasures of bridge, marbles and chess were enjoyed at the resort during these years, and championship tournaments were held in the Breakers Hotel. There was no way to replace the onetime draw of vaudeville acts, but dancing became increasingly popular; and now that radio and the movies were national institutions, Cedar Point promoters used these media to entertain the resort's visitors. During one season, "Freckles" Ray, one of the members of Hollywood's "Our Gang" comedy team, stayed at the hotel with his parents and gave daily performances. Later, Faulkner's Marionettes imitated the stars of radio and the silver screen in the auditorium. The promotional spirit that seemingly had died with Boeckling was returning to Cedar Point.

Other new events and activities were initiated during the 1930s. Perhaps the most innovative of these was the Ohio Band Camp, a respected educational and recreational program conceived by Peter F. McCormick. Director of Bands at Cleveland's West Tech High School, McCormick had proposed the idea of a camp for high school musicians to Boeckling in 1931. The concept appealed to Boeckling, for the camp would not only guarantee that the Cedars Hotel would be partially filled for eight weeks, but the band could also provide free entertainment at the resort. Despite Boeckling's death, McCormick proceeded to recruit teachers for the program, many from the Cleveland Orchestra. The camp that opened in 1932 drew students from many states for an intensive and carefully regulated schedule of excellent musical instruction and recreational activities. In addition to private lessons with renowned teachers, the students could be part of a concert band, marching band, orchestra and chorus. Even aspiring drum majors found professional training under the direction of Baldwin-Wallace College's Irene Kvetko. Each morning the camp's band marched to the pier for a flag raising ceremony, followed by concerts in the early afternoon and on Sunday nights in the rotunda of the Breakers. Uniformed in sailor caps and summer white, the camp band was soon in demand for concert appearances in locations as far away as Detroit and even Canada. Within a few seasons, the band was scheduled to provide regular weekly broadcasts on a number of NBC radio stations. Not only did the band camp provide publicity for the resort, but many of its graduates went on to receive scholarships to major conservatories, later becoming teachers and professional musicians. The Ohio Band Camp remained a distinctive part of the Cedar Point scene until McCormick elected to discontinue the program after the 1944 season.

As the economy started to improve, Cedar Point again attracted large numbers of conventions, excursions and company outings. Fred Long established a number of nationality days, such as the All-Ohio Irish Day, which were designed to attract large crowds from throughout the state. Sandusky Day, a longtime tradition each August, attracted as many as 15,000 local people for a day of picnicking, games and contests. Major prizes such as washing machines and radios appealed to families who had not been able to afford

such luxuries during the Depression. Industrial picnics often brought immense crowds, and in 1935, when Akron's B.F. Goodrich Company selected Cedar Point for its annual "Play Day," a crowd of 40,000 was anticipated. Many of the Akronites arrived in six train sections of fourteen passenger cars each, while another 1500 rubberworkers sailed on the *Goodtime* from Cleveland and thousands more arrived by car.

The convention business was given a major boost when the old Cedar Point Convention Hall was air conditioned and modernized. Business blossomed, and in 1934, the American Legion selected Cedar Point for its large state gathering. Other statewide meetings, including the Elks, the Grotto and the Ohio Teachers, similarly looked with favor on the resort's accommodating management and extensive facilities. A unique feature of the annual Ohio Liquor Dealers' conference was a huge block of ice with four red roses frozen inside that was displayed in the lobby of the Breakers—an exhibit provided by the distillers of Four Roses Whiskey. At the 1933 meeting of the 308th Engineers Association, an area of Cedar Point called Pump House Park was rededicated as Engineers' Park in honor of the 1921 founding of the World War I veterans group at the resort. Despite the fact that Cedar Point had become slightly dingy and somewhat worn-looking as a result of the economy, the convention business remained strong from the mid-1930s through the 1940s.

A perennial concern of Ed Smith's was the effect of the Depression on mass transportation systems. Because many people could not afford to own or operate automobiles during the 1930s, maintaining lines of transportation to the peninsula was a matter of survival. Even though the railroads were saddled with their own financial problems, many, like the Baltimore & Ohio, attempted to stimulate passenger business by offering low cost excursions to Cedar Point. In Sandusky, Ed Smith freely distributed complimentary passes for passage on the *Boeckling*, and the cost of a season pass for the steamer was held at one dollar throughout most of the decade. In addition, speedboats or "water taxis" were added in 1933, to provide twenty-four hour service between the Sandusky docks and the resort.

Smith's greatest transportation concern, however, was the financial instability of some of the steamship lines that operated daily from Cleveland, Detroit and Toledo. The Cleveland & Buffalo Transit Company, which had acquired the Cleveland route in 1914, and had placed the beloved *Goodtime* in service in 1925, had been in financial trouble for a number of years. Although the Cedar Point route might have been profitable, the C & B Line was losing money on its three big steamers that maintained overnight service between Cleveland and Buffalo. After some years of struggle, the line abandoned all service after the 1938 season. The *Goodtime*, too old and worn to be of much value to other steamship lines, was sold and scrapped a few years later. Fortunately for Cedar Point, the Detroit & Cleveland Navigation Company, who operated one of the largest passenger fleets on the lakes, expressed an interest in the old Cleveland-Cedar Point and Put-in-Bay route. Although they could not make all of the arrangements necessary to start operating on Cedar Point's opening day of the 1939 season, the D & C Liner *Eastern States* was assigned to the route in July and was retained in this service throughout the 1942 season.

The Toledo route suffered problems similar to those of the C & B Line's Cleveland service, and the *Greyhound*, which had been placed on the run in 1925, was withdrawn from service in 1931. During the following summer, there was no Toledo service; but in 1933, the *Put-in-Bay* operated out of Toledo on certain days of the week. The Detroit route handled by the *Put-in-Bay* was financially more stable than the other route, but when the *Put-in-Bay* added Toledo as a port-of-call, the number of weekly sailings from Detroit was reduced. It was clear by the late 1930s that Cedar Point would not be able to rely on the lake passenger steamers for many more seasons.

The threat of losing valuable steamship service was not the only concern that faced Ed Smith. In 1938, rumors circulating in Sandusky claimed that the G. A. Boeckling Company had been unable to service its debts and that the Cleveland bank that administered the Boeckling Trust had offered to sell the entire peninsula to the State of Ohio for $3,000,000. Smith promptly denied the rumors, but it was a fact that after Boeckling's death the resort's poor earning record had made the trust almost worthless. The sale of Cedar Point would have placed more than half of the receipts from the sale in the trust and, consequently, the trust would have produced the yearly charitable funds for which it had been established. The sale never materialized, probably because of an unwillingness on the part of the State, rather than any desire on the part of the trust officers to retain resort ownership. It became clear to Ed Smith that if a future sale of the property was to be averted, some sort of a profit-generating miracle was needed. Just such a miracle arrived in the form of the Big Band craze that swept the country after the mid-1930s. Although Cedar Point was a little slow to enter the Big Band market, the operators approached this newly found source of income with great vitality.

During the winter of 1938-39, the upper level of the Coliseum, which had recently served as a skating rink, was once again converted to a ballroom. When the Coliseum's dance floor first opened in 1906, the ballroom was anything but glamorous. The original

paint scheme was dull, the lighting was nothing more than bare light bulbs, and no attempt was made to decorate the cavernous hall. The newly redecorated ballroom, in stark contrast to the original dance area, was so glittering that even straight-laced Ed Smith described it as "breathtaking."

The new ballroom was an art deco showplace. All of the ceiling trusses and supporting pillars were covered, and soft, indirect lighting was mounted on each of the pillars which surrounded the dance floor. From the ceiling, a series of multi-tiered rainbow-colored lights cast a soft magical glow on the dancers as they glided across the wooden dance floor. At the northern end of the building, a large stage with a rainbow-motif backdrop and colored lighting was installed, while at the opposite end, scores of tables and chairs were provided. The new refreshment menu offered sandwiches, along with a full selection of beer, wine, champagne and liquor. Later, concessionaire William Balaun added a cigar and cigarette counter. The newly redecorated ballroom at Cedar Point was not only one of the largest in the Midwest, it was also among the most beautiful.

Ed Smith was admittedly shocked by the rates that the dance bands were charging, but he spared no expense in bringing the top headliners to Cedar Point's ballroom. The new dance floor opened on June 10, 1939, to the music of Don Bestor's Orchestra, who was followed by weekly engagements of the bands of Shep Fields, Russ Morgan, Ozzie Nelson, Blue Barron, Eddie DeLange, Clyde McCoy, Glen Gray, Vincent Lopez, Buddy Rogers, Bob Zurke, Henry Busse and the "Waltz King," Wayne King. While these great "radio bands" hosted thousands of dancers in the ballroom, smaller "house" bands were engaged to play dance sets at the hotel's Terrace Tavern.

Because Cedar Point booked only the most popular of the national bands, the ballroom was an instant success. Advertising for the ballroom appeared in newspapers as far away as Pittsburgh, and the arrival of dancers from distant cities helped boost the sagging hotel business. By July, the art deco dance hall had become so famous that NBC arranged to carry live broadcasts from the Cedar Point ballroom on 103 of its affiliated radio stations, and the sounds of the resort's bands were heard coast-to-coast each week. When Ted Weems and his young vocalist Perry Como arrived in June of 1940, radio broadcasts from Cedar Point had gained such a large listening audience that station WTAM featured live Big Band shows several times a week. During the heyday of the great dance bands, the Cedar Point ballroom was open seven nights a week and on Saturday afternoons. The sounds of a famous dance band drifting out over the lake and the bay created one of the more romantic eras at Cedar Point; but even more importantly, those romantic sounds drew crowds whose generous spending helped to save the ailing resort.

Most of the bands that were booked into the ballroom stayed at the Breakers; and after the ballroom closed each night, many of the bandsmen drifted over to Fred Posner's Castle Sandwich Shop. Posner's hot corned beef sandwiches and cold beer were a welcome treat after a night on the stage, and after eating, the musicians enjoyed informal jam sessions at the Castle. Posner became friendly with many of the bandleaders, and his hospitality was known in the band world from coast-to-coast. By the early 1940s, the walls of the Castle were covered with autographed photos of Bob Crosby, Benny Goodman, Woody Herman, Clyde McCoy and dozens of other musicians who appreciated his cordiality. In fact, Posner's affable nature went well beyond providing a late night gathering place for the band members. When the celebrated black trumpeter Roy Eldridge arrived at Cedar Point for an engagement, the white members of the band took rooms at the Breakers. But long-standing segregation policies, common at most American resorts in the 1940s, denied rooms to blacks. The sympathetic Posner offered Eldridge a bed in a room at the Castle, and soon the trumpeter's autographed photo was added to the Castle's collection.

Late in the 1941 season, the operators of the steamer *Put-in-Bay* featured Cedar Point in their newsletter, stating that "The parade of youth and beauty on the boardwalk at Cedar Point rivals Atlantic City in attractiveness, and the pure white sands of the beach are thronged by health seekers throughout the day enjoying a glorious sun bath." Travel publications described the beach as the finest between the Atlantic and Pacific Oceans, and it seemed that Cedar Point's magical reputation was returning. In fact, just after the July 4th holiday of 1940, Ed Smith joyously declared that both management and concessionaires were happier than he had seen them in many years.

Just at a time when the resort was able to forget the Great Depression and look forward to a brighter future, America entered World War II. Many resorts and parks, especially those located near large cities or military installations, found that the inconvenience of war restrictions was more than offset by fast-spending crowds. Few of the concessionaires at New York's Coney Island could complain about business during the war years; but resorts like Cedar Point were located far from major population centers, and the effects of wartime restrictions induced an economic catastropohe. Unlike World War I, which was of short duration, the four years of World War II forced the government to impose many restrictions which adversely affected Cedar Point. Not only was the resort denied large quantities of food service supplies like meat, sugar and coffee, but it was also virtually impossible to obtain most maintenance and construction materials. The scarcity of paint and other supplies, declining attendance, and travel restrictions were all factors that reduced Cedar Point to a decaying relic by war's end.

As the opening day of the 1942 season approached, Ed Smith's principal concerns were the changes that transportation restraints might force upon the resort. Both tires and gasoline were rationed, and Smith anticipated that fewer automobiles would be seen in the parking lots. To counteract this, he negotiated with the railroads in an attempt to increase the number of Cedar Point excursions and talked with bus companies about starting coach service to the resort.

Many Great Lakes steamships were placed in government service, and it was not known in early 1942 if any ships would be available for the Cedar Point route. Meetings with the owners of the *Eastern States* and *Put-in-Bay* relieved some tension, however, when they assured Smith that neither vessel had been requisitioned by the government. Both companies were able to maintain regular service in 1942, but ticket sales were disappointing. On some weekdays, the *Eastern States* left Cleveland with less than 100 people on her decks, and although weekend ticket sales sometimes approached 2,000, it is clear that the D & C Line was losing money on the Cedar Point route. After Labor Day, the line informed Ed Smith that the *Eastern States* would be needed in 1943 to replace vessels that had been acquired by the navy. Smith's frantic efforts to replace the D & C Line failed, and 1943 was the first year in almost forty that a passenger steamer did not operate between Cleveland and the resort. A year later, however, a Cleveland company was formed to revive the route, and the old steamer *Theodore Roosevelt* maintained service for two summers. Although the ship's owners claimed to have carried 100,000 passengers in 1944, it does not appear that the *Roosevelt* was able to operate profitably.

The dwindling attendance of the war years also affected the Sandusky-to-Cedar Point route of the resort's Bay Transportation Company. Even though the *Boeckling* had a large passenger capacity, it had always been necessary to use two or more boats on the route. After 1941, however, only the *Boeckling* was needed to handle the smaller crowds. Not since 1887 had the resort trade been serviced by a single vessel.

The war also brought many other changes to Cedar Point. The annual "Sandusky Day" celebration adopted a patriotic theme, and war bonds replaced appliances as the day's prizes. War Bond Drives became commonplace events, and in 1942, one of these drives featured an appearance by the comedy team of Abbott and Costello. Patriotic feeling was naturally accompanied by hostility toward America's enemies. The

Japanese String Game, and other concessions that had been operated for decades by Japanese-Americans, were the targets of vicious verbal attacks. The Japanese games were quickly closed, and their entire stock of fine china and porcelain prizes was purchased by game operator Tony Anast. But Anast immediately discovered that players who won prizes marked "Made in Japan" angrily smashed them on the ground.

After the close of the 1942 season, it was revealed that the army was considering the conversion of the Breakers into a military convalescent hospital. The G.A. Boeckling Company announced that if the conversion took place, the resort would not be open to the public in 1943. The Breakers, however, lacked the heating system needed for the winter months, and the army lost interest. The only result was that the army's late-spring decision forced the resort's opening back until late June in 1943.

The war economy did provide a few new opportunities for business at Cedar Point. The defense industry had created thousands of new jobs in the Midwest, and Cedar Point attempted to attract business from these plants by launching an advertising campaign that extended as far as three hundred miles away from Sandusky. The effort proved somewhat successful. The Jack & Heinz Company, a defense contractor located near Cleveland, selected Cedar Point as part of their employees' recreational program. Each week, the company sent fifty employees and their families to Cedar Point, providing rooms at the Breakers, an allowance for meals, and fifty dollars to be used on the midway and for various attractions. But whatever new business was obtained from the defense industry was more than offset by stringent gasoline restrictions that severely limited automobile travel, and thus, reduced attendance. By 1943, government inspectors were lurking in the Cedar Point parking lots, ready to issue citations to motorists who were caught violating the non-essential driving regulations. Faced with answering these charges in court, most would-be resort visitors elected to remain closer to home. The result was sparse crowds, especially noticeable on July 4th and Labor Day, which were usually thronged with guests. In fact, the only resort visitors who were unaffected by travel restrictions were the crews of U.S. Navy training vessels that occasionally anchored off the peninsula and operated launches to the resort.

Cedar Point's concessionaires were forced to deal not only with the dwindling crowds, but also with many difficulties in obtaining supplies. At William Balaun's coffee shop in the Breakers, eggs were usually available for breakfast, but it was impossible to offer bacon, sausage or other meats. Most sandwich meats were also scarce, and Mrs. Balaun became a wizard at producing a tasty ham salad from canned hams. Her ham salad sandwiches emerged as the

resort's best-selling sandwiches of the war years. The Balauns, like most of the die-hard concessionaires, made the best of a bad situation. On the beach, they rented inflatable rubber rafts that had been declared surplus by the navy. At their cigar counter in the Breakers, the Balauns occasionally had the opportunity to offer cartons of cigarettes or boxes of navy surplus Hershey Bars. Each sold for two dollars a box and the limited stocks sold quickly, with many Sanduskians making the trip to the resort solely to buy these scarce items.

Not every concessionaire was able to cope with the wartime problems, however, and in the spring of 1942, Ed Smith was busily seeking new concession operators. Among those that he could place immediately were a horoscope reader, a roller skating rink operator, and someone to manage the bridle paths. Surprisingly, new concessionaires did sign contracts with Smith during the 1940s. On the midway, Secondo Berardi installed the Octopus ride in 1941, and two seasons later, he added the Tilt-A-Whirl. By the 1950s, his sons, Albert and Eugene, would own and operate many of the park's rides. Other rides were added, including the Flying Skooters, the Roll-O-Plane, and the patriotically named Yankee Bullet. After the High Frolics coaster stopped operating in 1940, the resort was left with only one coaster, the Cyclone. William Balaun considered constructing a coaster of unique design to replace the High Frolics, but the declining attendance figures gave him second thoughts.

New shows and exhibits also made an appearance during the war years. Renee J. Zouary, whose father had long operated the fun house, brought his Bouquet of Life show to the resort a few seasons after it closed at Cleveland's Great Lakes Exposition. Described as an "embryological exhibit of the story of life," the Bouquet of Life's mystique was enhanced by a policy that refused admission to anyone under twenty-one years old. On the site once occupied by the High Frolics coaster, Zouary also installed his well-known Monkey Speedway. Here, twenty-six monkeys raced miniature electric cars at speeds reputed to reach forty-five miles per hour.

William J. Balaun, the successful Akron restaurateur who ran the hotel coffee shop and cigar counter, expanded his concessions during the war. Among his operations were cigar counters in the Coliseum, a series of souvenir stands, the Beachcomber refreshment stand along the beach, a game room in the hotel, and all of the beach concessions, which included both raft and swimsuit rentals. Each summer, Balaun moved his entire family into one of the resort's old cottages, and everyone helped run the stands. Even his youngest son could be seen in his baby carriage behind the hotel's cigar counter. At the Castle

Sandwich Shop, Frederick Posner finally gave up his concession in order to devote time to his family's meat business in Cleveland, but the operation was immediately acquired by Irving Ross and his wife. For the next 30 years, Ross' foot-long hot dogs and hot corned beef sandwiches were a Cedar Point tradition. In 1942, Albert Berardi and Howard Berni, both sons of concessionaires, built a french fried potato stand on the midway. A year later Albert's mother arrived on the peninsula to help with the stand. Affectionately known as "Momma" Berardi, she made the family's fresh-cut french fries an institution at Cedar Point, while at the same time befriending scores of college students working at the resort. Often, when payday was still a few days away and funds were running low, Momma Berardi dispensed free bags of her delicious french fries to many of the student workers. Just like Coffelt's fudge and Ross' hot dogs, Bernardi's french fries became synonymous with Cedar Point.

Even though a number of new concessionaires arrived at Cedar Point during the 1940s, the atmosphere of the resort remained mostly unchanged. The pace of life at Cedar Point was unhurried. Ed Smith and August Kuebeler, Jr. leisurely rode bicycles around the grounds. And, despite the availability of more modern methods, the resort still ran its old fashioned bottling plant in a corner of the Coliseum. Every day college boys refilled bottles with four or five flavors of soda; and every morning at eight, refreshment stand manager, Charlie Sutter, loaded an old truck with cases of freshly filled bottles and delivered them to the company's half dozen beverage stands. It was this resistance to change, coupled with the poor economy of the 1930s, as well as restrictions of the war years, that reduced a once great summer resort to an outdated, crumbling, dingy facility...one with a very questionable future.

The attractive entrance to The Chaussee as it looked during the 1930s and 1940s.

Follett House Collection

The Administration Building and the cigar and postcard stand, 1930s.

Follett House Collection

After Prohibition was repealed, the Lobby Tavern in the Breakers Hotel became a popular retreat.

Follett House Collection

Edward A. Smith directed Cedar Point through the difficult years of the 1930s and 1940s.

Polly Smith Collection

When the dining room was redecorated in the popular art deco style, it was renamed the Green and Silver Grill.

Hayes Presidential Center/Frohman Collection

Entrance to the Green and Silver Grill (right) and the Cafeteria Moderne, 1930s.

Cedar Point Archives

**Irene Kvetko leads the
drum major class at the
Ohio Band Camp, 1937.**

Dorothy Staker Collection

**Students from the Ohio Band
Camp canoeing on the lagoons.**
Irene Leeds Collection

The shady and colorful Terrace Tavern at the Breakers Hotel offered cocktail service and nightly entertainment.
Cedar Point Archives

During the 1930s, the popular *Put-in-Bay* handled the resort routes from both Detroit and Toledo.

Institute for Great Lakes Research/
Bowling Green State University

From the wheelhouse of the *G. A. Boeckling*, a typically small crowd of the 1930s is seen leaving the pier en route to the resort section.

Cedar Point Archives

The Eden Musee wax museum's facade showing the wear that was typical of Cedar Point buildings during the 1930s.

Toledo-Lucas County Public Library

Installed in 1934, the Tumble Bug was one of the few rides added to the Amusement Circle during the Depression.

Cleveland Press Collection/Cleveland State University

In the spring of 1934, the midway is prepared for the mid-June opening day. At the extreme right is the loading station of the High Frolics coaster which debuted that season.

Cleveland Press Collection/Cleveland State University

In need of repair and facing declining patronage, the Leap the Dips coaster was closed and razed during the mid-1930s.

Andrew Vettel Collection

A view from the lake during the late 1930s shows the bathhouse on the right, the Cyclone on the left and the first hill of the High Frolics coaster in the center.

Cedar Point Archives

The "back curve" of the Cyclone coaster in 1934. Inside the coaster's structure are the steel parking garages that were built in the mid-1920s.

Center for Archival Collections/Bowling Green State University

The magnificently remodeled art deco ballroom on the second floor of the Coliseum, 1939.

Alden Photographers, Sandusky

Frederick Posner (center) behind the bar of the Castle Inn that he operated from 1932 through 1941.

Dick Posner Collection

The lobby of the Breakers Hotel in 1940. In the center is William Balaun's newsstand and souvenir counter.

Hayes Presidential Center/Frohman Collection

One of the larger rooms in the Breakers Hotel in 1941. The wicker furniture had been part of the furnishings since the hotel's 1905 opening.

Hayes Presidential Center/Frohman Collection

The Flying Skooter ride was installed by Secondo Berardi in 1944.

Rosanne Berardi Collection

The Rocket Ships, operated by Roy Parker's Concourse Amusement Company during the war years.

Follett House Collection

Surplus navy life rafts were rented on the bathing beach by William Balaun during World War II.

John Balaun Collection

A portion of the Amusement Circle just north of the beach about 1940.

Follett House Collection

The initial plunge of the Cyclone coaster. By the 1940s, rotting wood suggested the resort's desperate financial condition.

Follett House Collection

A typical midway game of the 1940s being operated by Florence Stinson and Albert Fresch.

Albert Fresch Collection

Coffelt's original salt water taffy stand, 1940s.

Coffelt Candy Company

The Moon Rocket, which, due to poor business conditions, spent only a few seasons at Cedar Point.

Albert J. Tedaldi Collection

The Cleveland-Cedar Point Steamship Company's *Theodore Roosevelt* at the lake pier in 1945.

Follett House Collection

Cracked concrete walkways leading from the bay pier were evidence of Cedar Point's declining fortunes in 1943.

Cedar Point Archives

The quiet picnic groves near the Coliseum had remained mostly unchanged since the early 1900s.

Cedar Point Archives

William Balaun's Beachcomber stand was located along a boardwalk that was much in need of repair by 1940.

John Balaun Collection

The lagoons and bridle paths contributed to Cedar Point's relaxed atmosphere during the war years.

Cedar Point Archives

The Amusement Circle, looking toward the beach, showed signs of a decade of neglect and declining business.

Hayes Presidential Center/Frohman Collection

Motorcycle riders in front of the dangerous motordrome concession, early 1930s.

Cedar Point Archives

In 1934, the Chaussee was the only road that led to the resort. In the distance is the legendary Cyclone roller coaster.

Cedar Point Archives

Pilots Bill Long and Al Baker offered sightseeing flights from the Cedar Point beach during the early 1930s.

Cedar Point Archives

Henri Rigo came to Cedar Point in 1927 and remained the resort's popular head chef throughout the 1930s.

Authors' Collection

Off-duty dining room employees relax in front of the beachside refreshment stand during the summer of 1937.

Authors' Collection

The Man Killer From India Show, a temporary exhibit of the1930s.

Toledo-Lucas County Public Library

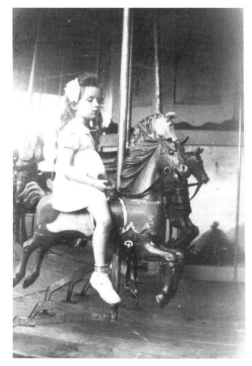

Gasoline-powered trains carried visitors from the lake pier to the main resort area.

Toledo-Lucas County Public Library

The daughter of a Cedar Point concessionaire riding the small carousel that operated near the beach during the early 1940s.

Sheila Stanley Ehrhardt Collection

The Cyclone, the Ferris Wheel and a small, portable carousel as seen from the beach.

Follett House Collection

A section of the midway showing the Yankee Bullet (left) and the Custer Cars (right).
The domed building is the Penny Arcade.

Follett House Collection

The Flying Skooter ride, with Noah's Ark in the background.

Follett House Collection

The *Eastern States* operated from Cleveland to Cedar Point from July, 1939, through the 1942 season. Here, she prepares to leave Cleveland's East 9th Street Pier.

Authors' Collection

By the 1940s, the turn-of-the-century cottages beyond Hotel Breakers were shabby and in need of paint.

John Balaun Collection

A canoe and a rowboat on the lagoons. To the right of the lagoon is the bridle path.

Cedar Point Archives

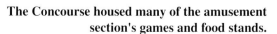

The Concourse housed many of the amusement section's games and food stands.

Follett House Collection

On hot summer days, the beach was a sea of people from the eastern end to Hotel Breakers.

Cedar Point Archives

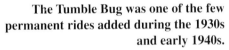

The Tumble Bug was one of the few permanent rides added during the 1930s and early 1940s.

Cedar Point Archives

The eastern end of Cedar Point's famous beach as viewed from the roof of the bath house.

Follett House Collection

Chapter Eight

On the Road to Recovery

At the close of World War II, Cedar Point was in deplorable condition, and recovery seemed hopeless. Ed Smith had become so pessimistic about the resorts's survival that he discouraged concessionaires from making major investments or buying new equipment. Despite the best efforts of Smith and the concession owners, twenty-five years of declining business and neglect had exacted a costly toll on Cedar Point's appearance.

Guests arriving at the peninsula during the late 1940s were immediately aware of the resort's sad condition. Those who debarked at the lake pier were greeted by an old and rotting dock in need of major rebuilding. But such repairs were never contemplated, for steamship service to Cedar Point from the various cities was, itself, nearly extinct. On the Cleveland route, the owners of the *Theodore Roosevelt* had failed to turn a profit in 1945, and the following season the run was assumed by the aging ex-cruise ship *Alabama*. She, too, could not be operated profitably and was replaced in 1947 by the *Cadillac*, which proved to be unsuitable for use on the sometimes choppy lake. After a year without passenger service, the D & C Line tried running their *Eastern States* and *Western States* on alternate days in 1949, but the close of that season brought an end to the Cleveland-to-Cedar Point route that had been initiated by the *Eastland* in 1907. Passenger service from Detroit employing the *Put-in-Bay* had been suspended after the 1948 season, although she continued to offer limited service from Toledo until 1951. When the *Put-in-Bay's* whistle signalled her last departure from the lake pier, the era of the big passenger steamer was ended at Cedar Point.

Those who crossed Sandusky Bay on the *G. A. Boeckling* were immediately aware of the large billboards fastened to the steamer's sides . . . an indication of desparate attempts by management to generate revenues by renting advertising space. The *Boeckling*, however, still presented a pretty fair ap-

pearance after a recent coat of fresh red and white paint. On her decks passengers still enjoyed the hand-dipped ice cream bars sold by young boys carrying ice chests. Running with the resort ferry were Worthy Brown's seven shiny Chris Craft speedboats which gave fast taxi service between the Sandusky pier and the peninsula.

The trip across the bay was a pleasing, even exhilarating, experience; but when visitors stepped off the gangplank at Cedar Point, they were met by badly cracked cement walkways dotted with patches of grass and weeds growing wild. To the left of the main pier was the almost vacant Cedars Hotel with its 1930s coat of white and green paint noticeably peeling. Not far beyond the Cedars was the Crystal Rock Castle, now equally shared by Ross' lunchroom, an ill-equipped first aid station, and a fire department comprised of two ancient and barely serviceable trucks. Behind the Castle were the lagoons and the bridle paths, two of the few resort attractions not in need of repair. Both were still charming, romantic and naturally beautiful.

From the lagoons, it was a short walk to the Breakers Hotel, once the pride of the resort but now showing the ravages of age and neglect, despite the best efforts of veteran hotel manager Tom Sabrey. The screens on the windows were rusty and full of holes, the mattresses were old and uncomfortable, an overwhelming mustiness permeated the entire main floor, and the wings of the building were infested with families of racoons. The lobby, however, maintained a respectable appearance, due primarily to the neatly-kept cigar counter of William Balaun and the gift shop of Abe and Ann Buckholtz. The operation of the Buckholtz family had been expanded during the late 1940s when they installed a small toy shop in the lobby. In the Terrace Tavern, white-shirted college boys with black bow ties still worked as waiters. Although they tolerated low pay and bleak dormitories, tips at the Terrace were usually generous, and each year the students returned to Cedar Point.

In front of the hotel stretched that magnificent beach . . . still among the finest in the country. Along the beach and the boardwalk a few changes were taking place. Between the beach and the hotel ten lighted horseshoe pits were built in 1949, to accomodate an interstate tournament. In addition, several metal plaques were placed along the beach to commemorate events from Cedar Point's illustrious past. In 1948, a committee headed by Sandusky's pioneer aviator, Reinhardt Ausmus, unveiled a plaque honoring the 1910 Curtiss flight. A reenactment of the flight was also planned, but the committee dispensed with the formality of landing at the resort. During the following summer, the Notre Dame Club of Cleveland posted a plaque dedicated to Knute Rockne. This event attracted enough interest to warrant the appearance of a Movietone camera crew to film the ceremony for movie theatre newsreels.

During these years, a leisurely walk along the Cedar Point boardwalk would take the stroller past the resort's old vaudeville theatre, as well as the convention hall. On Sundays, the theatre was used as a chapel, but attendance was low, and proceeds from the collection plate seldom covered the visiting clergy's weekly travel expenses. Consequently, concessionaire William Balaun initiated the unique idea of "renting" pews to worshipers to help defray the cost of the services.

The convention hall, too, was still in use. Many convention groups maintained their loyalty to Cedar Point, and a few new post-war meetings such as the AMVETS were also attracted. Other special events took place in the hall, including a 1949 dog show which attracted fifty-two breeds, 300 dogs and over 1000 spectators (an Irish Setter from Shaker Heights, Ohio, was awarded best of show).

Cedar Point's acclaimed dining room, now called the Green and Silver Grill, continued its tradition of excellence. Broiled lake trout, whitefish, filet mignon, Delmonico steaks and grilled lamb steaks highlighted the list of the restaurant's daily specials. Diners, however, were scarce, and often only a small portion of the large grill was in use. On some days, the college girls who were employed as waitresses would work an entire shift without serving a single meal. For these waitresses, employment at Cedar Point during the 1940s was often a discouraging experience. Their pay was only two dollars a day (about the cost of an average meal in the grill); they were served tasteless food in the employees' cafeteria and were required to wash their own uniforms in a laundry area between the two main dormitories. With few customers and a partially closed dining room, the waitresses had little hope of supplementing their low salaries with tips; but working at the resort and enjoying the beach during

off-duty hours could be fun, and many of the waitresses continued to work at Cedar Point for several seasons.

After the war, the Coliseum remained an active ballroom, and in 1946, eleven of the nation's best known dance bands appeared at the resort. But by 1948, the Big Band Era had come to an end and the dance crowds diminshed. The big ballroom was soon losing money. In an effort to reduce costs, Ed Smith closed the Coliseum's huge second floor ballroom and opened an intimate "social plan" dance floor on the lower floor. Small, relatively unknown, bands were engaged, and the price of dance tickets was lowered. But the new "social plan" dancing drew even fewer dancers, and the main ballroom was reopened in 1949. For the next few seasons, important bands like Tex Beneke and Ray Anthony, as well as singers such as Mel Torme, were booked. Although crowds may have been adequate, they could not compare with the throngs of dancers that had flocked to Cedar Point during the early 1940s.

Because of the efforts of individual concessionaires, the amusement section of Cedar Point survived the war in somewhat better condition than the rest of the resort. So weak was the roof of the old Eden Musee wax museum that, in 1947, a heavy snowstorm collapsed a large portion of it and damaged many of the exhibits. The owners had little incentive to make repairs, and the museum was sold to Ed Schmid, a well-known supplier of fun houses and dark rides. Schmid removed the wax figures to a Columbus warehouse where they were painstakingly restored. He then hired Mr. and Mrs. Fred Yost, who had managed the museum during the 1930s and 1940s, to supervise the restoration of exhibits at Cedar Point. After eliminating long-forgotten figures like Lord Roberts and William Gladstone, Schmid was able to open a much modernized Eden Musee a few seasons later. During the 1950s, Schmid also acquired Coney Island's New York Eden Musee, and the wax figures obtained in this purchase allowed him to periodically change the exhibits in the Cedar Point museum.

The wonderful Cyclone roller coaster had been very much neglected during the war, and in 1946, the G. A. Boeckling Company hired veteran coaster engineer Andy Vettel to oversee a complete rebuilding of the ride. Despite minimal maintenance during the war years, the Cyclone was still among the best coasters in the Midwest. Thrilling as ever, the Cyclone regularly inflicted bruised ribs, black eyes and even chipped teeth on those brave enough to ride her. Each morning ride manager Charles Egger made it a point to walk around beneath the Cyclone's structure, where he recovered money, jewelry, eyeglasses, wallets and even an occasional pair of false teeth . . . all jolted from their owners' possession by the vicious ride.

Very few new rides appeared on the resort's midway after the war's end, but in 1946, one daring concessionaire installed a Moon Rocket ride. After two discouraging seasons, the ride was offered for sale. A more successful ride installation was the new midway carousel which opened in 1946, replacing the original 1906 carousel that had been removed by its owners, the T. M. Harton Company. The replacement carousel was originally built by carver Daniel C. Muller and had operated for many seasons at Revere Beach, Massachusetts. At the suggestion of Ed Smith, Carl F. Holzapfel and his son, Richard, purchased the elaborate carousel from Revere Beach's Hurley family. Richard traveled to the East Coast to supervise the dismantling of the ride and its placement in railroad cars for shipment to Sandusky. When the carousel opened, the riders were greeted with beautifully carved horses and chariots, as well as an elaborately carved ticket booth resembling a Roman chariot.

Dotting the midway area in the late 1940s was the customary assortment of games, food stands and merchandise counters. George Donan's English Lavender, Ray Dirks' jewelry and Doc Gould's household gadget stands all occupied tiny buildings along the midway. In another small stand was Mary Miller, the quintessential gypsy fortune teller. Costumed in traditional long satin skirt, gold earrings, and colorful scarf, Mary the Gypsy gazed into her crystal ball and, for a small fee, predicted the future for wide-eyed customers. The games along the midway had changed very little, except that a Sandusky law of 1946 forced the closing of the very profitable and usually questionable gambling concessions.

One innovation that did appear on the midway after the war was Alden Ehrhardt's helium balloons. Years before, hydrogen-filled balloons had been sold along the midway, but pranksters with cigarettes had caused many disturbingly loud, if minor, explosions. During the war, both rubber and helium were in short supply, and children of the war years had never enjoyed the pleasures of a lighter-than-air-balloon. Consequently, Ehrhardt and his roving employees sold thousands of the colorful balloons, both on the midway, and at the steamer docks.

Among the more successful refreshment stands along the midway were Berardi's French Fries, Santi's Waffles, Finkler's Frozen Custard, Ericson's Popcorn and Ross' Hot Dogs. But very few new concessionaires wanted to challenge the business slump at Cedar Point, and the only notable addition to the midway was the Spaghetti Hut, opened by Frank Murru and Secondo Berardi in 1947. Spaghetti dinners were served in the "hut" for 75¢ and the new restaurant became popular with both resort guests and employees.

During one season in the late 1940s, a college stu-

dent working at Cedar Point penned an unofficial employee's anthem that began, "So this is Cedar Point, what a dismal joint." Little did that would-be poet know just how dismal the situation had become at the resort. When management announced a crowd of only 10,000 on July 4, 1949, it was an admission of gloomy business conditions. On Labor Day of that same season, the resort was swept by wind, rain and cold temperatures. Rough lake conditions made it impossible for the Cleveland steamer to dock, and the hotel had an occupancy rate of only thirty percent on a weekend that was normally overflowing. In August of 1946, rumors that a polio epidemic was raging at the resort raced through Cleveland and Toledo. Consequently, attendance at the resort deteriorated rapidly during a month that was always the peak of the summer season.

Through bad weather, lessening crowds and alleged polio epidemics, Ed Smith always maintained an outwardly optimistic attitude. But if the news media believed Smith's rosy predictions for the coming seasons, the concessionaires knew better. On one rainy day, the Berardis sold only nine ten-cent bags of french fries. Often, games took in no more than six or seven dollars in an entire day. For operators who were paying rent of forty or fifty dollars a week, such meager incomes were devastating.

The directors of the G. A. Boeckling Company were painfully aware of the situation. By 1947, they already viewed Cedar Point's position as hopeless, and the shareholders authorized the directors to sell the resort. The company's earning record had been so bleak since 1931, that it is not surprising that no buyer was located. Over the next few years, unfounded rumors of new owners constantly circulated in Sandusky. At one point Billy Rose, the successful owner of the Aquacade, was thought to be a possible buyer. Later it was thought that Cleveland Indians' owner Bill Veeck would acquire the property. As these rumors flourished and the directors searched in vain for a legitimate buyer, conditions worsened. By the end of the 1949 season, it was clear that the company would be incapable of paying off the bank loans that had been obtained to finance the opening of the season. The G. A. Boeckling Company was on the verge of declaring bankruptcy.

At the same time that the company was forced to inform its creditors that it could not service its debts, Ed Smith wisely announced his retirement. For forty-five years, Smith had known Cedar Point intimately and had witnessed both the resort's rise to fame and its more recent decline. Replacing Smith would be difficult, for he not only headed the Boeckling Company but as general manager was in charge of daily resort operations. The immediate task was to elect a new president, and the search for someone to fill the vacancy ended when one of the directors convinced B. G. Zeiher to accept the position. Bernie Zeiher was, at that time, serving as Solicitor of the City of Sandusky. Although he had no training in resort management, he was no stranger to Cedar Point, for his wife was a niece of George Boeckling. The events of the next half-dozen years would prove that Zeiher's abilities were equal to the challenges posed by a decaying summer resort.

Zeiher's position as the new president was not an enviable one. The Boeckling Company had lost money consistently for years, and in 1949 that loss reached $129,000. Not only could the bank loans not be repaid, but the owners of common stock had not received dividends for seventeen years. Tackling the immediate problems, Zeiher replaced the resort's archaic bookkeeping system with modern accounting methods. And, to reduce costs during the winter months, all but a few of the company's employees were laid-off in January of 1950.

In the meantime, the directors realized that selling the property was unrealistic and turned their attention to leasing the resort operation to a qualified person. Finally, a member of the board of directors convinced hotel owner Torrence C. Melrose to lease the resort for a ten-year period. The reluctant Melrose knew little of the resort business, but he possessed a flourishing chain of hotels that stretched from Cleveland and Toledo to Las Vegas. In fact, during the original lease negotiations, Melrose proposed closing the midway and concentrating on the hotel, beach and dining room facilities. Fortunately for the resort's many concessionaires, Melrose entrusted the details of the lease to his able lieutenant, Daniel M. Schneider. Although also a hotel man by trade, Schneider recognized the potential of the entire resort, and the midway dodged destruction. By February of 1950, the lease had taken shape and had been approved by the resort's directors. While the G. A. Boeckling Company agreed to spend $50,000 to improve the entrance road, Melrose was required to pay all insurance premiums, taxes and operational costs. The basic rental fee for the property was set at $25,000 for 1950, and $50,000 for the following year. During the remaining eight years of the lease, Melrose-Cedar Point, Inc. was required to pay the G. A. Boeckling Company eight-and-one-half percent of gross receipts. In addition, Melrose agreed to surrender one-half of the entrance and parking lot fees and one-half percent of the operating profit to Zeiher's company. Even though these terms were acceptable to both parties, a group of resort shareholders sought to legally block the lease. A temporary restraining order was issued by the court, but by early spring, the order was lifted and the lease executed.

Melrose's first important task was hiring a management team to operate the resort. Not surprisingly, he selected Dan Schneider as general manager. After years of experience in Melrose's hotel chain, Schneider was proficient in both finance and management. In addition, he was a highly ethical man who quickly won the admiration of everyone at Cedar Point. Since Schneider knew nothing about amusement parks, he approached an old friend, Edward S. Starr, and offered him the job of park manager. An experienced showman, Starr had once owned a dog act that toured amusement parks, and more recently, he had been a manager with Dailey Brothers Circus. Like Schneider, Starr was a hard-working professional who would contribute much to Cedar Point's recovery. Understanding that the operation would demand an active publicity department, Melrose and Schneider hired William H. Evans, a public relations specialist and ex-newspaperman, to handle convention and picnic bookings, advertising and publicity. For the next twenty years, Bill Evans would be the voice of Cedar Point. Having filled these positions, Melrose turned to his greatest interest, the Breakers Hotel. Jerry Johnson, a soft-spoken southerner, was hired as hotel manager. Serving under Johnson was a top-heavy staff of assistant managers recruited from the ranks of Melrose's acquaintances in the hotel business. If an economically efficient operation was Melrose's goal, it was not evident in his over-staffing of the hotel's front desk.

Because of the delay in finalizing the lease that was caused by the shareholder action, Melrose had only a few months to prepare for the 1950 season. Melrose withheld any announcements about improvements that he envisioned until May, and even then he cautioned that the rebuilding of Cedar Point would be a painfully slow process which might take many seasons to complete. But, he stated, a "new era" had begun and the changes would soon become evident.

On the evening before the June 16 season opening, Melrose invited newspaper, radio, hotel and travel representatives to tour the resort and see the improved conditions firsthand. The most obvious change was a gaudy new color scheme that had been applied to all of the main buildings. Dan Schneider hired a Toledo painting contractor and instructed him to paint everything a bright orange with white trim. Most of the resort managers and concessionaires complained that the new color was garish. Schneider agreed, but insisted that no visitor would be able to tour the resort grounds without realizing that painting and repairs were being accomplished. More subdued colors, he reasoned, would not capture their attention.

Since the Breakers Hotel had been built before the widespread use of the automobile, a road leading to the hotel was unnecessary at the time. Even after automobile travel became prevalent, the company, for some reason, never added a road; and guests were sometimes forced to carry their baggage from the parking lot or the docks. Melrose ended this inconvenience by constructing a road that led to the hotel's main entrance. This new roadway passed close to the old Crystal Rock Castle, and to avoid danger to pedestrians, Irving Ross' lunchroom was moved from the Castle to a new location on the midway. On the beach, Melrose installed floodlights for night bathing, and a sand cleaning machine was purchased to help keep the beach spotlessly clean. In the bathhouse, steel lockers replaced the old baskets that had been used for clothing storage for a number of years. The Coliseum dance hall was renamed the Crystal Ballroom, and circus acts were engaged to provide free entertainment just east of the Coliseum. On the midway, any games that smacked of gambling were evicted, and several new food stands were opened. Melrose also hoped to begin construction of a marina, but those plans would be delayed for a few years. In the Green and Silver Grill, Chef Joseph Yacovella, formerly of Melrose's Tudor Arms Hotel in Cleveland, presented a Thursday evening buffet featuring his famous "Blue Ribbon Beef."

The 1950 season opened with meager crowds, but as word spread that Cedar Point was being revitalized, attendance blossomed. Evans' deluge of publicity attracted thousands of curious visitors, and even celebrities like baseball's Bob Feller were seen at the resort. Of course, the larger crowds were welcome, and, instead of closing the resort after Labor Day, Melrose extended the season by hosting the Erie County Fall Festival in September. Reminiscent of a county fair, this event required that the garages be converted to livestock stables; and the Coliseum became an exhibit hall for farm and commercial products.

The improvements and new policies invoked by Melrose, combined with the public relations campaign of Bill Evans, had begun to reverse Cedar Point's years of decline. But, by the end of the 1950 season, it was clear that Melrose was losing interest in the resort, and his attentions were again turning to his chain of hotels and a horse farm in Kentucky. To his closest business associates he confided that he was anxious to terminate the lease, and in the fall of 1950, it appeared that Cedar Point's rebirth would be short-lived. In the meantime, Dan Schneider had developed a personal interest in Cedar Point and expressed a desire to assume the remaining nine years of the lease. Since the G. A. Boeckling Company had no objection to this plan, Melrose departed and Schneider became the president of the newly formed operating company, Cedar Point, Inc.

For Schneider and his wife, Betty, the assumption of the lease was laced with hardships. Unlike Melrose, they were not financially supported by a chain of pro-

fitable hotels. Living in the old Hermitage and often working sixteen hours a day, Dan Schneider tirelessly converted the decrepit Cedar Point into a wholesome family resort, while Betty devoted her energies to improving the floral displays, painting, and sprucing up the grounds.

Schneider's first offical action was to eliminate the top-heavy hotel management team that Melrose had created. The staff of managers and assistants was replaced by Sam W. Gerstner, an experienced hotel man who had most recently supervised the Tudor Arms Hotel. Gerstner not only took on the responsibility of running the big hotel, but he also supervised the Green and Silver Grill, now renamed the Coral Dining Room, and the cafeteria. After a few years, Gerstner was able to lure executive chef Frank Cavano from one of Cleveland's finest restaurants. Directing a kitchen staff of sixty, Chef Cavano also prepared dining room menus and managed large banquets. For some of these banquets, Cavano personally created intricate ice carvings to serve as table centerpieces.

Working throughout the winter months, Gerstner sought to restore and modernize the Breakers. Hundreds of rooms were repainted, rusted window screens were replaced, and old worn mattresses were discarded. Under Gerstner's direction, the Breakers once again became a respectable hostelry.

Even though Schneider had no background in managing a huge resort complex, he had definite and practical plans for Cedar Point. A major objective was to transform Cedar Point's rather tarnished image into that of a clean, wholesome family entertainment center. At first he emphasized fundamental improvements: the painting of neglected buildings, re-cementing cracked walkways, improving the parking lots, expanding the picnic groves and adding charcoal grills. Cars from the trams that once ran to the lake pier were converted into small picnic shelters. A chapel was built above the Coral Dining Room, and Betty Schneider kept the altar adorned with fresh-cut flowers.

Keeping the resort guests entertained became one of Schneider's main concerns. Free movies were offered every night in the Coliseum, and parents considered it a blessing when a child care service was established in the hotel. While dance bands were still booked for the ballroom, small musical groups and Country & Western bands were featured on the Coliseum's lower floor. The policy of free circus acts was expanded, and everything from the Great Wilno's cannonball act to aerialists, high-divers and dog acts appeared near the midway.

In the Amusement Circle, changes were also evident. The saddest occurrence was the razing of the Cyclone roller coaster, a measure that became necessary when the costs of rebuilding the neglected ride exceeded Schneider's limited budget. For the first time in more than half a century, Cedar Point was without a roller coaster. But elsewhere on the midway, more encouraging events took place. Most of the rides owned by Roy Parker's Concourse Amusement Company were sold to Albert Berardi, who added several rides. At about the same time, Albert J. Tedaldi and Ida Berni purchased the miniature railroad. Tedaldi later owned the Rocket Ships, the Laff-in-the-Dark and the Loop-O-Plane. Tedaldi and Berardi eventually emerged as the owners of most of the midway's amusement rides. Through the efforts of the concessionaires and Ed Starr, the midway was expanded and modernized during the 1950s. For thirty years, most of the park's few kiddie rides had been scattered around the Amusement Circle and little effort was made to cater to the younger children. But the post-war "Baby Boom" brought new money-making opportunities, and in 1952, Schneider and Starr convinced Leonard Jefferson to open a ten-ride Kiddieland section. In addition, Renee Zouary installed a unique indoor bicycle ride, allegedly the only one of its kind in the United States. And, the Great Western Express, a jeep disguised to look like an old fashioned locomotive, was purchased to haul carloads of guests from the ferry dock to the midway.

With the objectionable gambling games gone, new family-oriented games and shows dominated the Amusement Circle. In 1955, Ed Starr built an air conditioned Fascination game with seats for forty players. Nearby, a children's fish pond, a grocery wheel and a novel Shooting Waters game were opened. Doc Gould's wax figures portraying the Last Supper, and a machine that pressed the Lord's Prayer onto a penny also helped promote the new image of Cedar Point. Among other concessions that operated on the revamped midway were a shooting gallery, an archery range, a basketball game, a silhouette artist, horoscope readers, fortune tellers, handwriting analysts and an age-weight guesser.

The enthusiasm that Schneider and Starr displayed seemed contagious, and concessionaires began spending money to repair and repaint their stands. Some even built new stands or opened additional concessions. "Dutch" and Mary Biechele, who bought the frozen custard stands from Leo Finkler, rebuilt the midway stand and entirely replaced the stand near the beach. Their creamy custard, originally containing twelve percent butterfat, was declared by many to be the best in the world. The Coffelts built a new Carmel Corn stand out of glass blocks which produced a dazzling display of lights after dark. Hayden Fouts not only renovated his two souvenir stands, he also designed and installed an eighteen-hole miniature golf course east of the Coliseum. Like the shooting gallery,

Fouts' golf course stayed open late to entertain the couples who streamed out of the ballroom at intermission. Joseph and Florence Santi, who already operated the lagoons and several food stands, opened a boat and canoe rental on the beach. And, after working as refreshment employees for a number of seasons, Loyezelle Haffner, Georgia Manley and Don Good took over the refreshment stand on the ferry pier and renamed it Lomango Lunch. Here they served light lunches and assorted snacks to waiting passengers and employees. Everywhere on the midway new building fronts, fresh paint, modern signs and colorful lighting could be seen. And, for the first time in years, concessionaires were reporting profits.

In the Crystal Ballroom, the tradition of booking nationally known dance bands continued. Guy Lombardo, the Dorseys, Claude Thornhill, Ina Ray Hutton and Ray Anthony appeared on selected evenings, while lively polka bands played on Friday nights. Even if the Big Band Era was officially over, the ballrooom at Cedar Point continued to draw large numbers of dancers. This was good news for the college girls who worked as waitresses in the Coral Dining Room, because on especially busy evenings many of them were recruited to serve drinks in the crowded ballroom. It was hard work, but the college girls received an evening's wages of four dollars, plus a pocketful of tips from the free-spending dancers.

As Dan Schneider was quick to learn, the outdoor amusement and resort business is governed by a number of factors that are beyond the control of even the best manager, and the many forward strides he made during the 1950s were not without occasional steps backward. In 1952, still more rumors of a polio epidemic at the park, followed by a major steel industry strike, drastically curtailed attendance. In 1955, a record-setting heat wave brought business to a standstill; and two seasons later, consistently bad weather kept the crowds away from a peninsula which is especially unpleasant on cold and rainy days. But even though the weather did not always cooperate, Schneider, Starr, Evans and Gerstner succeeded in their efforts to revive Cedar Point. By 1955, the hotel was generating $266,000 in revenues, and the Coral Dining Room brought in an additional $215,000. A year later, annual operating expenses exceeded $1,000,000, which included a payroll of $350,000 for a seasonal work force of 600 employees. Attendance at the resort reached 760,000 by 1958, and even after the necessary improvement expenditures, Cedar Point, Inc. reported profits of $80,000.

The accomplishments of Schneider and his staff also returned the failing G. A. Boeckling Company to prosperity. By the mid-1950s, Schneider's annual rent had reached $100,000. The Boeckling Company's 1949 losses of $129,000 were reduced to $49,000 in 1950. A year later, these losses were further reduced to $4,000, despite the $30,000 that was needed for pier repairs. The revenues produced by the lease and by special projects developed by Bernie Zeiher allowed the company to repay old loans and return to its former solid financial footing.

Throughout the 1950s, one of Schneider's dreams was the revival of passenger steamer service from Cleveland, but so few passenger boats survived the post-war years that the plan was never feasible. Without the need for any alteration, the deteriorating lake pier was named "Fisherman's Wharf" and anglers were soon reeling in white bass, perch, and an assortment of other Lake Erie fish. But in 1957, the pier was badly damaged when it was struck by a lake freighter. Repairing the pier would have served little purpose, and Schneider simply posted a sign advising fishermen that they were using the pier at their own risk. On June 12, 1958, the rickety pier collapsed, dumping four fishermen into the still-cool lake waters, where they were rescued by the Coast Guard. A few years later, the pier's surviving pilings were removed with explosives, and the last vestige of the resort's once-thriving steamer excursions disappeared.

During the years of Schneider's lease, the G. A. Boeckling Company retained control of the ferry operation through its subsidiary, Bay Transportation Company. However, the aging steamer *Boeckling* was making it difficult to operate at a profit. Not only did she require constant maintenance and burn tons of coal, but a recent Federal law required that she carry a full complement of twenty officers and crew for each eight hours of daily operation. Bernie Zeiher and the company's directors faced a dilemma. The continued operation of the *Boeckling* would result in substantial financial losses, but the retirement of the beloved ferry would produce a public outcry. Sentimentality aside, the directors had a responsibility to the shareholders, and the retirement of the vessel was the only real option. After sailing more than 300,000 miles on Sandusky Bay, the last 100,000 under the command of Captain Otto Wyss, the *Boeckling* made her last trip on Labor Day of 1951. The following July, she was towed to a Wisconsin shipyard to be used as a floating warehouse. To replace the *Boeckling*, Zeiher contracted with an Erie boatbuilder for the construction of three sixty-five foot motor vessels based on the design of the sturdy and seaworthy Lake Erie fishing boats. The first of the trio, the *G. A. Boeckling II*, arrived in Sandusky in time for the start of the 1952 season and was christened by one of George Boeckling's sisters, Bertha. The remaining two boats, *Cedar Point* and *Cedar Point II*, were delivered in 1953. Under the command of Captain Wyss, the new boats not only provided the regular service to the resort, but during the pre-season spring months, they

also handled five-hour fishing trips on the lake. The hardiest of fishermen could even rent one of Cedar Point's old cottages, complete with cold-running water, for forty-two dollars a week during April and May. The modernization of Cedar Point's passenger fleet also erased the need for a separate operating company, and the fifty-year old Bay Transportation Company was dissolved. Thus, the boat line became the property of the G. A. Boeckling Company.

The retirement of the *G. A. Boeckling* and the construction of a new passenger fleet was a bold and aggressive action, but it was only the beginning of Bernie Zeiher's efforts to give the company new life. The erosion of much of Cedar Point's shoreline had been unchecked for years, and in some places the beach had been reduced from one hundred feet to a mere ten feet in width. To stem this destructive process and promote sand deposits, the company spent $50,000 to construct a series of sandstone jetties near the tip of the peninsula. Following this expenditure, and some major dock repairs, Zeiher turned his attention to the residential section of the peninsula, which had been more or less dormant since Boeckling's first effort to develop the area just before World War I. After more than forty years, the residential section was little more than crude summer cottages located on tiny lots. Believing that the time was right to redevelop this land, Zeiher borrowed $350,000 to improve the water supply, construct a water tower, and subdivide the land into larger lots suitable for year-round housing. By 1953, the company had sold 107 lots and generated $287,000 in revenues. While real estate agents continued to market these lots, the profits from the development of the residential area were used to finance Zeiher's most ambitious project.

Lake Erie steamship service and railroad excursions were, by now, just fond memories, and most resort visitors arrived by automobile. On busy days, the Chaussee was the scene of massive traffic jams and long delays. Traffic congestion was not only frustrating for the resort visitors, but also disrupted life in the residential section. The solution was to revive Boeckling's 1929 plan to construct a bridge from Sandusky's east side to the peninsula. In 1953, Zeiher announced plans to construct a causeway. Governmental approval of the plan was temporarily halted by a veto from Ohio Governor Frank Lausche, but the bill passed the Ohio Legislature and received the endorsement of the U. S. Army Corps of Engineers in 1954. Despite a price tag of $600,000, and a brief construction hiatus due to the bankruptcy of the contractor, the causeway was completed and opened on June 12, 1957. Although the forty cent toll collected from each car that crossed the bay generated substantial income, the causeway unexpectedly became the catalyst that changed Cedar Point's prospects for the future.

During its construction, the causeway stimulated the curiosity of Toledo bond dealer, George A. Roose, who regularly flew over the Cedar Point peninsula on trips to Cleveland where he was supervising a land development project. A graduate of Harvard Law School and the Chairman of Roose, Wade & Company, Roose was an astute businessman with a keen eye for prime residential property. Roose believed that converting Cedar Point into the "Fort Lauderdale of the North" could easily earn the developer of the land more than $2,000,000. After investigating the G. A. Boeckling Company, Roose quietly acquired two thousand shares of the company's stock . . . just under one-sixth of the outstanding shares. But, to assume control of the company, he needed to acquire the 6,260 shares of stock held in the G. A. Boeckling Trust. Consequently, in May of 1956, he offered slightly more than $250,000 for the shares owned by the trust. Since the trust had never been productive, the trustees favored the opportunity to convert the stock to cash for more lucrative investments and advocated the sale. Many of Boeckling's surviving relatives, however, felt that the price was too low, and they attempted to block the sale with legal action. The controversy was not resolved until the following February when Roose and a group of investors, including Emile Legros of the First Cleveland Corporation and Paul Dunn, acquired majority control of the G. A. Boeckling Company. Bernie Zeiher agreed to remain as president, but within a few years, Roose replaced Zeiher, and Emile Legros was elected chairman of the board.

In the midst of the Roose acquisition of Cedar Point, a statewide controversy erupted, protesting the potential owner's plans for the peninsula. Roose had made it clear that he was a land developer and not a resort operator. Once he gained control, the resort would be closed and most of the old buildings would be razed. In their place, a thousand expensive ranch-type homes would be built. But thousands of Ohioans had sentimental feelings for the resort, and their influence extended as far as the State Capital in Columbus. The State was already considering the purchase of Chippewa Lake Park in Medina County, and many newspapers urged the purchase of Cedar Point as a new state park. By June of 1956, Governor Frank Lausche declared that if any attempt was made to convert Cedar Point into a residential community, the State would purchase the property in the interest of public safety and the public well-being. An eight-man legislative committee, chaired by Representative F. K.

Cassel, was established to study the feasibility of a state acquisition.

The controversy seemed to cool briefly when Cassel's committee realized that Schneider's lease did not expire until December 21, 1959. Consequently, no action was required for several years. Eventually, Cassel's committee urged the State to purchase only the undeveloped tip of Cedar Point, citing the fact that the Department of Natural Resources was ill-equipped to assume control of a park as large as the resort area. Furthermore, the practical Cassel cautioned the state legislature that the purchase price of the entire peninsula could be as high as $7,000,000. Nevertheless, Lausche asked for the appropriation of $1,500,000 and assured Ohioans that, if it became necessary, the State would condemn the property and purchase Cedar Point for a "fair" price. By December, the "Zuber Plan" introduced by Representative Lytle Zuber, recommended the purchase of only the 100 acres occupied by the hotel and the amusement section.

Faced with the loss of their investment and of future revenues, Roose and Legros decided to cancel plans for residential development. Instead, they made public their intention to develop Cedar Point into the "Disneyland of the Midwest." With the announcement that Cedar Point would remain a recreational facility, the State ended all plans to purchase the peninsula, and the stage was set for the remarkable metamorphosis of Cedar Point.

Roose and his partners now owned the resort, but they made no attempt to end Schneider's lease. Instead, they used the 1957 and 1958 seasons to develop the plans that would become effective when they assumed active direction of the resort. An architectural firm was retained to create plans for the first phase of the resort's redevelopment, and Robert McKay, formerly manager of Buckeye Lake Park, was hired to supervise new construction projects. In 1958, a stone breakwall was built to provide the protection necessary for a proposed marina that was envisioned as a major part of the first new phase of development.

After two seasons of planning, Roose and Legros were anxious to get started on the new Cedar Point, and they purchased the reamaining year of Schneider's lease. Dan Schneider and Ed Starr remained as consultants during the next few years, and their decade of experience at Cedar Point proved invaluable to the new owners. With the assumption of the Schneider lease, the way was clear for the most amazing transformation ever seen in the outdoor amusement industry.

The new carousel, brought to
Cedar Point from Revere Beach
in 1946.

Albert J. Tedaldi Collection

By 1948, the once pristine entrance to the Green
and Silver Grill exhibited peeling paint and rotting
wood.

Eleanor Brucken Collection

Berardi's Pretzel dark ride.

Rosanne Berardi Collection

"Momma" Berardi in front of the French
Fried Potato stand, late 1940s.

Rosanne Berardi Collection

Not suited to Lake Erie's weather conditions, the *Cadillac* served on the Cleveland-to-Cedar Point route only in 1947.

Great Lakes Historical Society

At the very end of passenger service to Cedar Point, the *Put-in-Bay* (left) and the *Eastern States* are seen at the lake pier in 1949.

Follett House Collection

In a building that was once a roller skating rink, Frank Murru and Secondo Berardi opened the Spaghetti Hut in 1947.

Frank Murru Collection

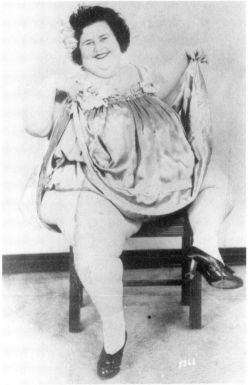

Dolly Dimples operated Cedar Point's side show during the late 1940s. Five feet tall, Dolly weighed 575 pounds and had a seven-foot waist.

Frank Murru Collection

The interior of the Spaghetti Hut in 1947. The restaurant's operator, Frank Murru, stands on the left near the cash register.

Frank Murru Collection

Cedar Point's ancient fire trucks parked in a section of the old Crystal Rock Castle.

Eleanor Brucken Collection

A group of the college boys who worked as waiters in the hotel's Terrace Tavern and Lobby Tavern, 1950.

Eleanor Brucken Collection

Daniel M. Schneider, whose faith in the resort started Cedar Point on the road to recovery during the 1950s.

Pat Gerstner Collection

A major part of Schneider's initial plans called for the painting of all of the resort's neglected buildings and statuary.

Eleanor Brucken Collection

Irving Ross' lunch stand in the Concourse building, 1950s.

Sally Leizman Collection

Bob Feller, one of the Cleveland Indians' greatest players, visiting Cedar Point in 1950.

Pat Gerstner Collection

Coffelt's new popcorn stand. The glass blocks of the building were colorfully illuminated at night.

Coffelt Candy Company

Lomango Lunch, a refreshment stand located on the bay pier during the 1950s.

Loyezelle Haffner Collection

Dutch Biechele's new custard stand.

Mary Biechele Collection

The old Concourse building, where most of the game stands and some of the refreshment stands were located.

Alden Photographers, Sandusky

Albert Fresch operating a cat rack game during the early 1950s.

Albert Fresch Collection

The newly redecorated fish pond game.

E. S. Starr Collection

Ed Starr's new Fascination game, mid-1950s.

Mary Biechele Collection

One of the new games of the 1950s was Ed Starr's grocery wheel . . . operated by longtime resort employee Doc Gould.

E. S. Starr Collection

After passenger ship service ended, the decaying lake pier became a haven for fishermen.

Hayes Presidential Center/Frohman Collection

The christening ceremony of the first of three new all-steel ferry boats, June 7, 1952.

B. G. Zeiher Collection

The retired *G. A. Boeckling* and the new *G. A. Boeckling II* at the Sandusky docks, 1952.

B. G. Zeiher Collection

The tug *John Roen IV* towing the *G. A. Boeckling* to Sturgeon Bay, July 10, 1952.

B. G. Zeiher Collection

Completed in 1957, the causeway eliminated traffic jams and reduced travel time from the mainland.

Cedar Point Archives

Edward S. Starr, the energetic park manager of the 1950s.

E. S. Starr Collection

The miniature steam train in Leonard Jefferson's Kiddieland.

Norman Sharp Collection

The Kiddieland roller coaster about 1957.

Norman Sharp Collection

The Laff in the Dark at night.

Norman Sharp Collection

The Kiddieland carousel, 1957.

Norman Sharp Collection

A 1950s view of the midway looking toward the beach. The funhouse is on the right.

Sheila Stanley Ehrhardt Collection

The tree shaded midway of 1956.

Cleveland Plain Dealer

Santi's boat rental on the lagoons.

Alden Photographers, Sandusky

The Coliseum and the old pagoda style restroom buildings in the late 1950s.

Alden Photographers, Sandusky

The entrance to the Coral Dining Room and the cafeteria in 1959. On the right is the Grand Pavilion.

Alden Photographers, Sandusky

The attractive passenger steamer *Alabama* was one of the last ships used on the Cleveland to Cedar Point route.

Follett House Collection

The pagoda-style post office was located not far from The Coliseum. Later, the building became the Pagoda Gift Shop.

Eleanor Brucken Collection

Berni's Penny Arcade was a midway landmark until it was razed in 1959 to make way for new construction.

Rosanne Berardi Collection

The entrance to the Pony Track, circa 1950.

Pat Gerstner Collection

In addition to his family's famous french fry stand, Al Berardi also operated the Pretzel dark ride during the 1950s.

Rosanne Berardi Collection

The Tilt-A-Whirl, Rocket Ship ride, and the Bouquet of Life show were midway fixtures of post-war Cedar Point.

Cedar Point Archives

Ballroom dancing in The Coliseum was continued after the end of the Big Band Era, but crowds were never as large as they had been during the 1939 to 1945 years.

Cedar Point Archives

One of the rides owned by Al Tedaldi, a major concession-owner of the 1950s.

Albert J. Tedaldi Collection

By the late 1950s, the Crystal Rock Castle was closed to the public and became the resort's maintenance shops.

Cedar Point Archives

The Holzapfel family, who owned and operated the carousel, kept the ride brightly painted and glowing with hundred of colored lights

National Amusement Park Historical Association.

The employee's cafeteria (center) was given the unsavory nickname "The Gangrene Room" by the seasonal employees.

Eleanor Brucken Collection

When this photo was taken late in the 1950 season, Cedar Point's midway had only one surviving roller coaster. Soon, the Cyclone would also be razed.

Bruce Young Collection

Chapter Nine

The Renaissance of Cedar Point

During the late 1950s the American amusement park industry was at an exciting crossroad. Immediately after World War II, the 400 amusement parks that survived the Depression were reporting revenues totaling $34,000,000. By 1958, 700 parks entertained 100,000,000 people and claimed receipts of over $300,000,000 per year. Disneyland, which opened in 1955, was an inspiration to an industry that had not experienced much innovation in over half a century. By the end of Disneyland's first season, Walt Disney could boast that his new park had taken in almost $10,000,000 and enjoyed pre-tax profits of over $900,000. But the business was also highly speculative and financially risky. During the next decade, many of the nation's greatest old-time parks—Riverview, Euclid Beach and Steeplechase among them—would close due to increased costs, soaring land values and a variety of urban problems. Even the trendsetting parks, however, found that success was not guaranteed. California's gigantic Pacific Ocean Park and New York's uniquely themed Freedomland were both doomed to failure. The average medium-sized amusement park could expect an income of about $218,000 in 1958, but the predecessors of the "super parks" were already predicting receipts in the millions and earnings of $600,000 per year. It was on this speculative, but potentially rewarding, segment of the industry that Roose and Legros set their sights.

It is evident that the new owners' plans for Cedar Point would deviate from the pattern established by Disneyland and the other new amusement centers. Initially, most of the company's investment dollars would be spent on the resort segment of Cedar Point, rather than the amusement section. But, since there was limited time to accomplish new projects for the 1959 season, it is not surprising that on opening day scores of workmen were still struggling to complete many of the construction projects. Concrete, poured only days before, was barely dry when the new admission gates were opened. The smell of fresh paint permeated the halls of the hotel. Everywhere on the peninsula it was apparent that $1,200,000 had been spent to initiate Cedar Point's renaissance.

A large portion of the investment dollars were allocated to rebuilding the 1920s pier and to the initial phase of the marina's construction, but improvements were also evident at the hotel and along the midway. At the Breakers, a colonial-style facade framed the new entrance, guest rooms in the Bon Air section were renovated, and a coffee shop and the Surf Cocktail Lounge were opened near the lobby. Much of the old metal statuary adorning the resort grounds was repaired and repainted. On the midway, where concrete replaced old dirt paths, new rides were installed. The Wild Mouse, a small roller coaster-type ride, and a children's automobile turnpike represented a major investment, but the most popular ride to be installed at Cedar Point in many years was the new Monorail. Designed and built by John Braziel, William Burse and Edward Everhart of Akron's Ohio Mechanical Handling Company, the ride had originally been installed and tested at Akron's Summit Beach Park late in 1957. When that park closed in 1958, the ride, considered the first commercial monorail in America, was moved to Cedar Point. Suspended nine feet above the midway, the gasoline-powered monorail engines effortlessly pulled five streamlined passenger cars around a three-quarter mile course. With its attractively landscaped entrance and futuristic appearance, the monorail produced more income than any other ride on the midway in 1959.

While these visible changes were being made to the resort grounds, Roose and Legros were also busy revising operating policies. Most of the new policies were not popular with concessionaires or Sanduskians, but they were necessary to assure a profitable resort operation. Season passes that provided for unlimited use of the ferry boats or free admission at the auto entrance had always been distributed freely to shareholders and scores of Sanduskians. The new management almost totally eliminated the season passes, requiring everyone to pay admission fees. A more drastic step, however, was the establishment of a long-range plan to ease-out concessionaires and eventually place all rides, games and food operations under the company's management. Owners of rides were urged to sell their equipment to the company, and faced with the alternative of eviction, most agreed to the sale. The old circular Penny Arcade, which had been operated by the Berni family since the 1930s, was torn down, and the company opened its own arcade on the lower floor of the Coliseum. All of the independent game owners were removed, and one major games concessionaire was given a contract to operate all of the resort's games. Most of the independent food stand operators remained for a number of years, but the resort's restaurants and new food stands were managed by Interstate United until Cedar Point's executives determined that they were ready to assume control of all food outlets and restaurants. One of the few concessionaires to resist the company's purchase offer was Ed Schmid, owner of the Eden Musee. Considering the offer of $125,000 far too low for the museum, he moved all of his wax figures into a storage facility near Columbus and left the resort's management with an old, empty building. Those few concessionaires who remained—the Berardis, the Santis, the Ross Family—made many major improvements to their food stands, and in some cases, built new stands.

The end of the 1959 season brought encouraging news. Both attendance and profits had increased, and banks, who only a few years before had considered Cedar Point a high risk, were now willing to make sizable loans to Roose and Legros. In an effort to sever all ties with the tainted reputation of "old" Cedar Point, as well as to better identify the nature of the company's business, the G. A. Boeckling Company was dissolved in March of 1961, and a new firm, Cedar Point, Inc., was formed. A public offering of stock was initiated, although a year later, eighty-eight percent of the company's stock was owned by the directors.

Some of the funds obtained from both the bank loans and from the sale of stock was slated to expand the marina. From the original 250 dock spaces, the marina evolved into one of the finest facilities on the Great Lakes; and by 1967, its docking facilities could accommodate 750 boats. On the pier, which was the center of the marina, the small lunch counter was replaced with the Marina Steak House, a marina store, a snack bar, a barber shop, a laundry, and ten individual baths for boaters. The impressive multi-million dollar marina was selected in 1960 as the site for the Cleveland Power Squadron's annual rendezvous and later became the location of the Great Lakes' largest in-the-water boat show. During the marina's

early development, the resort's management extended an invitation to the Tri-City Yacht Club to make the marina their headquarters. Having lost their clubhouse in a flood, the club readily accepted and, under the direction of Commodore Melvin Buyer, became the new Cedar Point Yacht Club. The club initially occupied and restored an old building near the marina, but later a new clubhouse was erected.

Additional funds were allocated to complete the restoration and modernization of the Breakers Hotel. Each season, more rooms were renovated and equipped with private baths, although as late as 1968 "economy rooms" were still available at low rates. These rooms, although clean and pleasantly furnished, were offered without televisions, air-conditioning or private baths. Northwest of the hotel, the twenty-two ancient cottages were in an advanced state of neglect and decay. Rather than attempting to renovate these cottages, management had them burned.

No sooner had the renovated hotel begun attracting guests than its management was accused of promoting a policy of racial discrimination. Since the early years of the century, Cedar Point, like every major resort, had excluded blacks from its hotels and cottages. Although Cedar Point had never attracted many blacks, the integration movement that became widespread in the 1950s inevitably reached the resort. During the summer of 1961, the NAACP lodged a complaint with the management of Cedar Point and requested that the outdated racial policy be abandoned. In complying with the request, one of the last vestiges of the old resort's policies disappeared.

By the early 1960s, Cedar Point was undergoing rapid changes. E. R. "Doc" Lemmon, a former Disney executive, was hired as general manager of the resort. The old Crystal Rock Castle, recently serving only as a maintenance building, was burned. The post office was closed, and its pagoda-style structure was saved from a similar fate when Mrs. Roose converted it into a souvenir and gift shop. The bathhouse where Knute Rockne had once worked was torn down, and in its place rose a new $50,000 bathing facility. The Hermitage, once the home of the winter caretakers, was razed, as was the old powerhouse. After the powerhouse smokestack was demolished, a new boiler house and maintenance center was built in its place. By the late 1960s, many of the resort's old rides and buildings had been removed or replaced. Those that remained—like the hotel, the Grand Pavilion and the Coliseum—had been completely refurbished.

When the steamer *Canadiana*, one of the last passenger vessels on the Lakes, was being considered for a revival of the Cleveland-to-Cedar Point route, plans were made to rebuild the lake pier, of which nothing more than pilings remained. However, when the route was not established, the last of the pier was removed. In Sandusky, the railroad spur that was used by excursion trains to reach the Cedar Point docks for more than eighty years was removed in 1961. Although Cedar Point's executives might have welcomed the revival of excursion trains, the railroad insisted that track maintenance costs far exceeded the minimal revenues that the spur would be capable of generating. Of Cedar Point's once extensive transportation network, only the bay ferry service remained in the 1960s.

If many people lamented the passing of old buildings and traditions, they still could not resist being impressed by the changes that came over the resort during the 1960s. Although the hotel and the beach thrived, it was during the 1960s that Cedar Point completed the transition from an old-time summer resort to a modern amusement park and entertainment complex. The entire midway section, which became larger with each new season, was fenced, and admission fees were initiated. Later, a "Pay-One-Price" plan allowed guests to obtain admission and the use of all rides and shows for one price. Despite some resistance to the new admission policies, revenues and attendance soared.

New rides that appeared on the expanding midway included the Rotor, the Dodgem, an eighty-five foot high Sky Wheel, antique Cadillac cars, a miniature frontier train, a live mule train and a western stagecoach pulled by live horses. By 1967, these and other midway rides helped Cedar Point to accommodate 50,000 riders an hour. As the managers started looking at more spectacular rides, efforts were made to buy one-of-a-kind or unusual rides from parks that had recently closed or were on the verge of closing. From New York's unsuccessful Freedomland, Cedar Point acquired two nicely themed dark rides . . . the San Francisco Earthquake and the Pirate Ride. From Cleveland's Euclid Beach Park, whose owners were already contemplating going out of business, Cedar Point obtained the unusual American Racing Derby. A fast variation of the carousel, this large ride had been built for the Cleveland park by Prior and Church during the early 1920s. Renamed Cedar Downs, the ride features rows of hand carved horses in out-stretched racing positions. The sleek horses glide back and forth in slots on a large circular platform that moves at exciting speeds.

For the younger visitors, one of America's largest kiddielands was built on the east side of the Coliseum after the miniature golf course was rebuilt on the opposite side of the building. Eventually, a full-size carousel became the centerpiece of kiddieland, and by the 1970s Cedar Point owned and operated four antique carousels . . . perhaps more than any other park in the world. The new midway stretched from the site of the old Amusement Circle of the Boeckling era to

the lagoons, and eventually it encircled the lagoons and reached the tip of the peninsula.

By this time, park management was concentrating on the acquisition of large, spectacular rides and attractions. The increases in attendance and resulting revenues made such a policy feasible, and as might be expected, the introduction of elaborate attractions stimulated even higher attendance. The first of Cedar Point's spectacular rides were the Western Cruise riverboat ride and the midway's Sky Ride. The Western Cruise was a logical way to utilize the old lagoons. The first boat was built by Bob McKay, who was forced, by budgetary restraints, to build the vessel from whatever materials happened to be on hand, such as old hotel bedsteads which were used to create decorations. As years went by, large amounts of money were spent to build highly attractive and authentic sternwheelers. Winding through many of the lagoon channels, the boats were piloted by college boys who gave running commentary as the vessels passed animated displays of wild animals, pioneers, log cabins and hostile Indians who fired rifles at the passengers. Passing a fort, simulated cannonballs caused geyers of water to erupt near the sides of the steel boats.

The Sky Ride, which was basically a Von Roll ski lift constructed on level ground, featured a number of four-passenger cars and ran from near the admission gates almost to the lagoons. Not only did this new ride eliminate a great deal of walking for weary guests, but it also afforded a magnificent view of the floral displays which became a trademark of the new Cedar Point. Like Boeckling before him, George Roose appreciated beautiful flowers, and he planned dozens of flower beds featuring intricate designs, many of which were clearly discernable only from the Sky Ride. By 1967, the Sky Ride was carrying 1,500,000 passengers in a season. Almost in the shadow of the Sky Ride and next to the midway carousel, the Mill Race debuted in 1963. In that year the flume ride concept was so new that Cedar Point's was only the second such ride in the world. Built at a cost of $300,000, the Mill Race was 1,230 feet long. Each boat was designed to resemble a hollow log, and the passengers were sent wildly careening through flumes of rapidly moving water. Near the end of the ride, the log boats were carried up a twenty-eight foot hill, then when descending the hill, the riders were unexpectedly splashed. Although flumes later became popular attractions at dozens of parks, the Cedar Point ride was considered a trend setting innovation in 1963.

One of George Roose's dreams for Cedar Point was the installation of an authentic narrow gauge steam railroad utilizing restored antique locomotives. Although he had already purchased an old locomotive, the board of directors rejected the idea of a railroad.

Undaunted, Roose and a group of investors obtained the board's permission to operate a steam railway as a concession, and the Cedar Point & Lake Erie Railroad was born. During the winter of 1962-63, construction crews moved over 6,000 cubic yards of earth, built trestles and a station, and by spring were laying track on the new roadbed. In the meantime, two old locomotives were reconditioned, and the line's original motive power included the "Maud L.," a 1902 engine from a Louisiana sugar plantation, and the 1911 "Albert." New steel passenger cars were fabricated, animated western figures were placed along the track, and the Cedar Point & Lake Erie Railroad carried its first passengers in 1963. After the 1966 season, the C.P. & L.E. was sold to the Cleveland Browns football club, but the ride was soon acquired by Cedar Point, Inc. Eventually, the railroad was extended from near the lagoons to the tip of the peninsula, and by 1968, six restored coal burning locomotives were needed to carry 1,500,000 passengers.

Within a few seasons, Cedar Point's management recognized the need for a large roller coaster. The first plans for a coaster were announced in 1961; and a year later, "Doc" Lemmon was investigating the costs of a dual-track racing coaster, but the construction of the first major roller coaster at Cedar Point since 1929 was delayed until the winter of 1963-64. The new coaster, named the Blue Streak in honor of Sandusky High School's athletic teams, was designed by veteran coaster engineer Frank Hoover. Throughout the winter months, crews worked in heavy winds and snowstorms to pour 559 concrete footers. Using three tons of nails and 200,000 feet of lumber they created a coaster seventy-two feet high and 2,400 feet long. Built on the approximate site of the old Leap the Dips coaster near the bay, the Blue Streak was a fine traditional wooden coaster that launched Cedar Point on the road to becoming the "Roller Coaster Capital of the World."

During the season that followed the unveiling of the Blue Streak, another unique and sensational ride was built near the beach. Only the fourth of its kind to be built, the Space Spiral was a 330-foot tower on which a sixty passenger revolving capsule traveled to an observation point over 200 feet above the midway. From this high vantage point, every part of the park and much of Lake Erie was visible.

In response to the new management's expansion program, the remaining food and game concessionaires replaced their old facilities with buildings that were appropriate for the glittering new midway. Near the admission gate, Irving Ross built a lunch stand to continue his tradition of foot-long hot dogs and hot corned beef sandwiches. Further up the midway, Joe Santi opened an old fashioned ice cream parlor and a barbecue stand, while Al Berardi began serving his famous fresh cut french fries from a new location.

The demand for Berardi's potatoes became so great during the 1960s that he was soon forced to stop serving Lake Erie perch sandwiches in order to devote all of the stand's fryers to potatoes. By the middle of the decade, Coffelt's taffy and fudge were sold not only along the main midway, but also in sparkling new stands near the Space Spiral. By the 1970s, most of these concessions had been acquired by Cedar Point, Inc. The last to be taken over by the park's management were the two french fry stands which, by then, were selling more than two tons of potatoes a day. In addition to the improvements in the area of food, the park's game concessionaire, Western Amusements, built a massive new complex that housed forty games behind a facade emblazoned by thousands of colored lights.

Even though the era of the great dance bands was technically over, the park's new management continued to book dance bands and major entertainers into the Coliseum for a number of seasons. In 1959, the Tommy Dorsey Band was a big hit, and the next year Glen Miller's Band proved that it was still a headliner. In 1961, ten well-known dance bands were scheduled, and some of these, including Guy Lombardo and Blue Barron, had been among the Coliseum's attractions twenty years earlier. The traditional band schedule was balanced by a more contemporary lineup of entertainers, including Brenda Lee, Al Hirt, Fats Domino and the Four Seasons. But Cedar Point's venture into the production of stage shows was not confined to the aging stage of the Coliseum. Lively musicals, presented in new facilities throughout the park, featured the talents of young high school and college performers. And it was these musical shows which captured the heart of modern-day park guests.

During this time, the old Eden Musee was removed, and the Hollywood Wax Museum was installed in its place. Although the Hollywood museum displayed life-sized figures of notable show business personalities, the figures were of fiberglass, not traditional wax, and largely unexciting. Turnstiles leading into the museum recorded disappointing patronage. After the 1969 season, the museum building was converted into the Centennial Theatre. Honoring the resort's 100th birthday, the Centennial Theatre offered original, well-directed musical shows. Along the midway, park guests were entertained by strolling musicians, including a hobo band, which added a note of fun and gaiety to a facility already brimming with "Something for everyone." By 1969, musical entertainment had become such a large part of the park's diversions that Cedar Point could justly claim that this was "where the Broadway Theatre Spends the Summer." During these years, Cedar Point, Inc. also became the owner of the Miss Teenage America Pageant, although the annual finals of this event were generally not held at the park.

People, however, were not the only performers at Cedar Point. Since its earliest days, the resort had offered animal acts and exhibitions. The new management was quick to recognize the potential for a high quality wild animal facility. Consequently, in June of 1964, they contacted the world renowned animal trainer, Lawrence Tetzlaff, and asked him to install a small petting farm-type exhibit of domestic and wild animals on the midway. Tetzlaff, known in show business as "Jungle Larry," was a highly respected zoologist, herpetologist and conservationist. Having developed an interest in snakes when a young boy, Tetzlaff studied at Western Michigan University and later joined Frank "Bring 'Em Back Alive" Buck as a collector of rare snakes and other reptiles for zoos and circuses. During World War II, he extracted venom from thousands of snakes to produce serums used to treat servicemen bitten by snakes in Africa and the Pacific. After the war, Tetzlaff adopted the name Jungle Larry, enlarged his personal zoological collection, and opened a wild animal show at Cleveland's Puritas Springs Park. When that amusement park closed, he moved to Chippewa Lake Park, and even became a well-known television personality.

Jungle Larry's small animal exhibit was an instant success, and during the winter of 1964-65, Roose and Legros induced him to move his entire collection of animals to Cedar Point. With the constant help of his wife, who was best known as Safari Jane, Jungle Larry created Safari Island on a strip of land bordered by the lagoons. Preserving as much of the wilderness as possible, he maintained a natural setting for animal enclosures and performance stages. Each season, he gave the island an authentic tropical appearance by placing Florida palm trees around the compound and hanging bushels of Spanish Moss from the trees.

Lions and tigers were usually Jungle Larry's most popular performers, but he also introduced acts that included leopards, jaguars, lepjags, chimpanzees, elephants, ponies, golden retrievers, poodles, llamas, alligators, birds, bears and tiglons. The tiglons, the result of mating a lion and a tiger, gained the world's attention when they were bred at Cedar Point in 1969. In addition to his outstanding arena shows, Jungle Larry installed a "Night Tunnel" where special lighting permitted visitors to observe rare and seldom seen nocturnal animals. During the first years of Jungle Larry's Safari Island, a small shop selling African carvings and a display of West African dancers were also among Tetzlaff's exotic offerings. By 1970, Safari Island was the summer home to more than 200 animals, and the annual feeding costs reached $60,000. In fact, the most popular time of day at Safari Island was often the evening feeding of the big jungle cats, each of whom consumed as much as twelve pounds of raw meat.

Unlike Disneyland, which developed as a series of themed park sectors, Roose and Legros never attempted to convert Cedar Point into a theme park, In 1968, however, the tip of the peninsula, near the site of the old passenger steamer pier, was developed into an area called Frontier Town. Literally carved out of the peninsula's undergrowth, this remote section of Cedar Point became a stop on the C.P. & L.E. Railroad and was also reached by the new Frontier Lift Sky Ride that operated from the main Funway. Frontier Town blossomed as a pleasant and attractive recreation of both the frontier west and small town America at the turn of the century. A saloon with traditional old west entertainment, an Indian village, a shooting gallery, themed food outlets, and a gift shop offered a quiet retreat from the noise and activity of the main midway. Before long, rides were added to Frontier Town. A second flume ride called Shoot-the-Rapids was built, and a magnificent Dentzel carousel was moved to Frontier Town from its home in Michigan. As the section expanded, the Cedar Creek Mine Ride roller coaster, another antique Cadillac car ride and other amusements were added. And, when the management became conscious of Cedar Point's colorful past, a museum of resort photos and memorabilia was installed in the Town Hall building.

During the 1960s, the enjoyable task of publicizing the exciting developments at Cedar Point was the duty of Bill Evans, one of the few remaining employees who had been part of "old" Cedar Point. By the time Evans retired in 1971, his legendary publicity stunts had earned him the sobriquet "The P. T. Barnum of Cedar Point." Evans not only obtained thousands of inches of newspaper publicity for the park, but was also the originator of many unique attractions and promotions that appeared on the midway. Beauty pageants, roller coaster riding contests and publicizing Jungle Larry's tiglons were among his efforts, but Evans was best known throughout the amusement park industry for the high school band event that he promoted on each season's opening day. Starting in 1962, Evans offered high school bands free admission tickets in return for taking part in a spectacular performance of massed bands. By 1967, the opening day event included 8,300 musicians from 105 high schools.

Evans was also involved in the creation of the Courtesy Corps, a group of attractive college girls who were selected to serve as hostesses and goodwill ambassadresses. Standing on raised platforms located on the midway, the Corps distributed maps, gave directions, assisted lost children, and helped make a visit to Cedar Point a rewarding experience. Although Roose and Legros were certainly the parents of the new Cedar Point, it was the promotional vitality of Bill Evans that catapulted the park into regional and national prominence.

During the years of Cedar Point's reconstruction, the park established a safety record that became the envy of the amusement park industry. Millions of guests were entertained without serious injury, but in 1968, the horses pulling the stagecoach suddenly bolted, upsetting the coach and injuring thirteen passengers. Always concerned for the safety of its visitors, the park immediately discontinued the stagecoach ride. Because of the peninsula's exposed position, weather was one factor that management could not control. In 1966, when heavy rains and high winds caused flooding, a temporary closing of the midway was necessary for the first time in the park's history. More serious, however, was the violent storm that swept into Ohio on the evening of July 4, 1969. Few of Ohio's outdoor entertainment facilities were spared. Many miles inland at Chippewa Lake Park in Medina County, dozens of falling trees crushed cars, and the rising lake water quickly inundated the park's midway. At crowded Cedar Point, the effects of the storm were even more disastrous. As trees were uprooted, a twenty-year-old man was killed near the Breakers. Stones and beach sand were hurled across the midway with stinging velocity. Thousands of park guests were caught out in the open. At Jungle Larry's Safari Island the big cat cages were smashed, but fortunately the animals were contained. Because of high water and fallen trees, hundreds of guests were unable to leave the peninsula that night. Interstate United provided food for the stranded guests, and the hotel lobby became temporary sleeping quarters, with the hotel staff distributing blankets in an effort to make the unexpected guests comfortable. Fortunately for Cedar Point, storms of the magnitude of the 1969 disaster are infrequent; and as George Boeckling pointed out almost seventy years before, the peninsula's spring and summer weather ranks among the most pleasant in the Midwest.

The changes that had taken place at Cedar Point in just ten seasons were almost unbelievable. Roose and Legros, capitalizing on the work started by Dan Schneider in the 1950s, had invested so much money that Cedar Point steadily evolved into one of the nation's greatest amusement parks. In 1961, after only three years of new management, *Time* magazine listed the park as one of the top seventeen in America. By that time, the operation had already grown so large that it required 930 telephones and a switchboard operated by nine college girls, to handle the park's daily communications. On one day in 1960, Bill Evans announced that a record 14,000 bathers passed through the bathhouse. Eight seasons later, an eleven mile traffic jam was created when 19,000 cars and 100 buses tried to reach the park. The parking lot had recently been expanded to accommodate 12,000 cars, but on busy days the roads leading to Cedar Point were so crowded that it became necessary for the park's own traffic control personnel to be stationed at the mainland end of the causeway.

Attendance figures grew steadily during the 1960s, and from the 760,000 people who visited the park during the last year of Dan Schneider's lease, the numbers climbed:

1959	970,000
1960	1,250,000
1961	1,525,000
1962	1,540,000
1963	1,500,000
1964	1,736,000
1965	2,000,000
1966	2,340,000
1967	2,555,000

By 1969, the park's combined rides carried a total of 31,427,408 riders in that single season. Yearly improvements that often exceeded $2,000,000 attracted even larger crowds, justified higher admission prices and stimulated in-park spending for food, games and souvenirs. From 1959 revenues of $1,338,807, the annual income figures shot upward to $18,000,000 in 1969. But as impressive as Cedar Point's performance was during the 1960s, it was merely a hint of what was to happen during the amazing 1970s and 1980s.

The fathers of modern Cedar Point . . Emile Legros (left) and George Roose.

Cedar Point

Installed in 1959, the Monorail was the midway's most popular ride for several seasons.

Alden Photographers, Sandusky

The mule train and stagecoach about 1960.

Alden Photographers, Sandusky

In 1960, the new midway included some of the older attractions such as the Eden Musee (left) and the domed arcade (right).

Alden Photographers, Sandusky

The Rotor, new in 1961, was located on the site of the old Amusement Circle.

Alden Photographers, Sandusky

The Wild Mouse was the first roller coaster-type ride at Cedar Point since the Cyclone was razed during the early 1950s.

Cedar Point

More of an illusion than a ride, the French Frolics lasted only a few seasons on the new midway.

Cedar Point

The Eden Musee's facade concealed fifty year old wax figures and an ancient midway building.

Cedar Point

The "1865" train was replaced in a few years by an authentic narrow gauge steam railroad.

Cedar Point

The Satellite Jets, originally located in the center of the park near the Coliseum, have remained popular through several decades.

Cedar Point

By 1963, the Sky Ride and large floral displays gave the midway a distinctive, new appearance.

Alden Photographers, Sandusky

One of the C.P. & L.E. Railroad's first locomotives, the Maud L., arrives at Cedar Point during the fall of 1962 . . . and awaits restoration.

A. A. Augustus Collection

Laying track along the new C.P. & L.E. right-of-way, 1963.

A. A. Augustus Collection

The restored Jennie K. crossing a bridge over the lagoons.

Cedar Point

When the Mill Race was built for the 1963 season, it was one of the first of its kind in the world.

Cedar Point

Cedar Point's Kiddieland section is among the largest in the United States. Behind Kiddieland is the Sky Ride and the Blue Streak roller coaster.

Cedar Point

The Blue Streak, which debuted in 1964, was the first major roller coaster built at Cedar Point since 1929.

Cedar Point

The Space Spiral inspired a new advertising slogan . . . "New Heights in Fun."

Cedar Point

Coffelt's new taffy, fudge and popcorn stand complex was built on a plaza at the base of the Space Spiral.

Coffelt Candy Company

Ross' modern refreshment building replaced the old Concourse lunch stand.

Sally Leizman Collection

A group of Irving Ross' employees serve his famous foot-long hot dogs.

Sally Leizman Collection

A typical line of customers waiting for Berardi's great french fries.

Rosanne Berardi Collection

"Momma" Berardi and her son, Albert, who had already sold more than 1,500,000 portions of french fries by the early 1960s.

Rosanne Berardi Collection

The new Shoot the Rapids ride in Frontier Town.
Cedar Point

Jungle Larry and one of his lion cubs sign a contract for the establishment of Safari Island early in 1965.
Nancy Jane Tetzlaff Collection

Jungle Larry and a baby elephant on Safari Island.

The Pirate Ride, a uniquely animated dark ride purchased from Freedomland for the 1966 season.

The Jumbo Jet, an all steel roller coaster, was located near the beach on the approximate site of the Cyclone coaster.

Cedar Point

The new Cedar Point . . . an aerial view during the late 1960s.

Hayes Presidential Center/
Frohman Collection

The old bath house being demolished to make way for a new structure.

Alden Photographers, Sandusky

From the 1950s until his retirement in the 1970s, Bill Evans was Cedar Point's promotional genius.

William H. Evans, III Collection

Although the Antique Cadillac Cars were installed during the early 1960s, the ride has remained a favorite for more than thirty seasons.

Cedar Point Archives

During the spring of 1965, the Space Spiral and a line of new refreshment stands are being hurried to completion.

During the first stage of marina construction, only two sets of docks were ready for boats.

The Bubble Bounce, because of its low rider capacity, lasted only a few years during the early 1960s.

Cedar Point Archives

Chapter Ten

The Amazement Park

The story of Cedar Point from the late 1950s to the 1980s is basically an evolutionary one. When Roose and Legros acquired the property in the 1950s, they found they were the owners of an old fashioned, fully equipped summer resort with a relatively small, adjacent amusement park section. Within a decade, Roose and Legros had developed their purchase into a first class amusement park, which, still another decade later, evolved into a virtually unequalled entertainment complex. The phenomenal growth of Cedar Point is reflected in the fact that the annual advertising budgets of the 1970s exceeded the gross revenues of an entire season in the late 1950s and early 1960s.

Perhaps the most visible change which occurred after 1970, was the replacement of many of the early 1960s rides with more modern and spectacular equipment. Continuously expanding their attractions and replacing older rides, Cedar Point retired the Wild Mouse, the original Rotor, the Sky Wheel, the Monorail, the French Frolics and a dozen other rides that had outlived their usefulness.

Less obvious to park guests were the upper management changes occurring within Cedar Point, Inc. George Roose and Emile Legros had been highly successful in guiding the resurrection of Cedar Point, but Roose was approaching eighty years of age, and both men were looking toward retirement from active management. Selected as their heir apparent was Truman B. Woodworth, who was appointed vice president in 1970. After twenty-two years with the Disney organization, Woodworth was a well-respected member of the amusement industry and was eminently qualified to direct Cedar Point through its second decade. Although Woodworth eventually resigned, he was, at one point, elected president when Roose stepped down to assume the less active role of vice chairman of the board.

With the retirement of George Roose, and the subsequent death of Emile Legros on January 1, 1975, Cedar Point entered a new stage of development.

Elected to the presidency of Cedar Point, Inc. was a new energetic leader, Robert L. Munger, Jr. No stranger to the Cedar Point operation, Munger, a Yale University graduate, was one of Cleveland's leading insurance executives. While searching for investments in 1960, Munger purchased stock in the fledgling Cedar Point company and was soon elected to the board of directors. After serving for four years as president, Munger's outstanding leadership was rewarded in May of 1979, when he was elected to the dual office of president and chairman of the board. Aggressive, knowledgeable and an experienced businessman, Munger was a fortunate choice to succeed Roose and Legros. Under his direction, Cedar Point reached a new pinnacle of development.

Much of the midway expansion that occurred after 1970, was directed toward the installation of state-of-the-art roller coasters. The first two new coasters built during these years were all steel: the Wildcat and the Jumbo Jet. The latter was erected on the approximate site of the old Cyclone coaster. Billed as the fastest coaster in the United States, the Jumbo Jet maneuvered seventy degree banks at high speeds, but still it was considered small in comparison to the coasters which followed within a few seasons. In 1976, the unveiling of the Corkscrew was a newsworthy event. Fast and smooth, the Corkscrew's trains negotiate a 360-degree loop before twisting through a corkscrew-shaped stretch of track that passes over the Cedar Point midway and the end of the lagoons. Loop-the-Loop coasters had been around since the early 1900s, but modern technology allowed for a safe rebirth of this type of ride, and the addition of the corkscrew section created one of the world's dynamic rides.

Two seasons after the Corkscrew debuted, Cedar Point spent $3,400,000 to install a gigantic coaster, which at the time it opened, was the tallest roller coaster in the world. Massive in comparison to the resort's once famous and feared Cyclone, the new

Gemini is a towering twin-track racing coaster, 3,935 feet long and a bone chilling 124 feet high. Not surprisingly, one of the Gemini's first riders was George Roose, then over eighty years old. Although retired from active management, Roose was still a familiar sight on the park's new rides. The imposing Gemini was built near the tip of Cedar Point and became one of the most noticeable features of the peninsula's skyline. On a clear night, its lights can be seen many miles out into Lake Erie.

The introduction of the Gemini paved the way for a whole new generation of coasters at Cedar Point . . . each with its own unique brand of excitement. Avalanche Run, an updated version of the 1920s Flying Turns coaster, uses sled-like trains that speed through curving troughs, creating the thrill of a bobsled run. The awesome Demon Drop made its appearance in 1983. Although perhaps not a coaster in the traditional sense, the Demon Drop features a 131 foot tower equipped with a high speed elevator mechanism that swiftly carries cars to the top. Hesitating only briefly, the cars then treat their riders to a fearful two and a half second, sixty-foot free fall that ends back at the loading platform. Computer monitored, and controlled by 103 electronic sensors, the Demon Drop is a technological wonder whose construction and operation would not have been possible at any earlier time in the history of amusement rides. Like all of Cedar Point's modern rides, Demon Drop presents a deliciously frightful appearance and promises an exhilirating ride.

Millions of dollars were spent installing roller coasters at Cedar Point, but the park's planning department did not neglect other types of rides. The showpiece of the 1972 season was the Giant Wheel, a German-built Ferris Wheel that rises 168 feet above the midway. Installed at a cost of more than $1,000,000, weighing 221 tons and illuminated by 32,000 colored light bulbs, Cedar Point's Giant Wheel is the most impressive ride of its kind since George W. G. Ferris amazed the public with his original wheel at Chicago's 1893 World's Fair. The wide acceptance of the two 1960s flume rides led to plans for additional rides of this type. In Frontiertown, White Water Landing replaced the more gentle Shoot-the-Rapids. Costing as much as a major roller coaster, White Water Landing takes its riders along 2,400 feet of water-filled channels before climaxing in a spectacular, if drenching, forty-five foot plunge. Four years later, in 1986, Thunder Canyon was built near Frontiertown. This ride provides the thrills of river rafting, complete with simulated rapids and a soaking trip under a waterfall. Riders should expect to emerge from Thunder Canyon thoroughly drenched and, accordingly, the park sells plastic raincoats near the ride's entrance.

Continuing the modernization program, the older rides of the 1960s were rebuilt, re-themed, and sometimes given new names. The Western Cruise at the lagoons enjoyed lasting popularity and, in 1970, it was equipped with new boats. During that season, Cedar Point's 100th year, the Western Cruise boats carried 1,500,000 passengers. The Cedar Point & Lake Erie Railroad, which Cedar Point, Inc. had purchased in 1967 for $600,000, transported an amazing 3,000,000 park guests in 1973. By this time, The C.P. & L.E. was one of the largest operating antique steam railroads in the country and included six restored locomotives, four engines in various stages of restoration, a switcher, complete engine shops and numerous passenger coaches. The park's carousel collection now numbers five, including Cedar Downs and a small kiddie merry-go-round. Each was painstakingly restored, immaculately maintained and, except for Cedar Downs, equipped with an antique band organ to provide traditional carousel music.

Cedar Point's inventory of rides has become one of the largest and most impressive in the country, but the planning department was always careful to balance the additional rides with new food stands, restaurants, games and gift shops. Among the restaurants are the hotel's Anchor Room and Coffee Shop, the Swiss Chalet on the midway and the Marina Steak House on the pier. The Coral Dining Room, the oldest restaurant on the peninsula, was closed when the Cedar Point Yacht Club's building was converted into the year-round Bay Harbor Inn. From lobster dinners at the Bay Harbor to the "fun foods" like taffy, french fries and hot dogs on the midway, Cedar Point's food service meets the challenge of providing a wide variety of good things to eat for as many as 3,000,000 visitors a year.

The rebirth of Cedar Point extended beyond the midway. In 1970, the park's ancient vaudeville theatre was razed but was barely missed due to the expansion of live show facilities throughout the park. Like the new rides at Cedar Point, the shows and exhibits became more costly and really quite spectacular in the 1970s and 1980s. In 1970, Sealand was opened near the beach. A walk-through marine exhibit, Sealand features eye-level windows that allow guests to peer into tanks housing dolphins, sharks, penguins and a wide variety of other aquatic animals. Later, Oceana debuted next to Sealand. A large, open-air marine stadium, Oceana uses Lake Erie as a natural backdrop against which expertly trained dolphins and sea lions delight spectators with their skillful antics.

By the mid-1970s, Jungle Larry's Safari Island had gained national acclaim, and he soon built a similar facility at Naples, Florida, which served as an ideal winter home for Cedar Point's animals. Gradually, the Cedar Point operation lost some of its wilderness-like appearance. Wider asphalt walkways, larger animal enclosures, a new entrance and an extensive gift shop were necessary to accommodate the large number of visitors who enjoyed Safari Island. The lion and tiger shows were still the main attraction, and in 1975, Jungle Larry constructed a new eighty-foot Chartersphere Dome with circular seating sections that placed the first row of spectators only five feet from Jungle Larry and his performing big cats. The proximity of the big cats added an element of excitement unique in the world of performing wild animals.

After Jungle Larry's death, the operation was continued by Safari Jane and her son, David, billed as America's youngest wild animal trainer. In 1986, Safari Jane carried on Jungle Larry's life-long dedication to educating the public about animals when she built Safari Canyon. Planned as an informal lecture area, the new feature is the perfect forum for introducing visitors to baby leopards, chimpanzees, snakes and other animals. The longest-running animal act in an American amusement park, Jungle Larry's African Safari is a lasting tribute to a man who will long be remembered as one of the world's great animal trainers, an advocate of animal training through kindness, and a master showman.

While Cedar Point's marine exhibits and Jungle Larry's African Safari were being further developed, Frontier Trail was cut from the thick underbrush that covered much of the land near the lagoons on the bay side of the peninsula. Connecting Frontier Town with the main midway section, the Frontier Trail was designed to afford a peaceful walk through a section of Cedar Point that is still heavily tree-covered. Along the trail, strolling guests will see many log cabins and themed buildings containing craft demonstrations, gift shops and food operations. Among the latter is a delightful confectionary where wonderful aromas invite the stroller to partake of freshly made taffy, fudge, cookies and other goodies. Farther along the Frontier Trail is a blacksmith's shop, a candlemaker, the children's petting farm, a fully-equipped glass blowing factory, an authentic grist mill (moved to Cedar Point from South Carolina) and a replica of Fort Sandusky. Near one end of the trail, a faithful reproduction of an old west dance hall offers draft beer, peanuts and, of course, entertainment by those legendary dance hall girls. Each year Cedar Point presents approximately sixteen live entertainment shows. The park's show directors annually interview and hire over 100 talented college students to perform as singers, dancers, musicians and other entertainers. A complete wardrobe department was formed to provide the vast array of costumes needed to produce shows that are changed yearly.

Although motion pictures had been a prominent attraction at Cedar Point during the early 1900s, they eventually lost their appeal and by the 1940s and 1950s were only secondary attractions provided for employees and hotel guests. By 1975, however, a Canadian corporation had developed a new giant screen concept, and Cedar Point took another look at the movies. The new IMAX system had been a great success at Expo 70, Expo 75, Ontario Place and Circus World, so the introduction of IMAX at Cedar Point was no surprise. To showcase their IMAX system, the Cedar Point Cinema, a 19,000 square-foot theatre with seating for 950, was built on the bay side of the midway, not far from the old Cedars Hotel. Through the use of a special projector and a sixty-seven by ninety foot screen, guests are awestruck by films that produce amazingly realistic sensations. In fact, when a film about flight was shown, some visitors complained of dizziness and vertigo.

For a number of years, Cedar Point's management had been considering the addition of attractions designed especially for their youngest visitors. Kiddieland and strolling costumed animal characters were the first attempts to entertain young children, but in 1985, a child's fantasyland was created in the building that had previously housed the San Francisco Earthquake ride. Bear Country, based on characters created by Stan and Jan Berenstain, includes a complete storybook bear habitat, a bear family tree house, woodland landscaping and a group of charming forest creatures that talk with the children.

Cedar Point's management has left no stone unturned in providing for the total comfort and entertainment of their guests . . . even the four-legged variety. Dogs are not permitted in the park itself; but, because many pets travel with their families, a "dogtel" was built in 1970, just outside the main gate with daytime-only facilities for forty-one lucky dogs!

The sweeping changes that took place on the peninsula between 1950 and the 1980s erased many traces of old Cedar Point. But, ever mindful of the park's rich heritage, management made a point of preserving and utilizing as many elements of the original resort as possible. Old iron street lamps, that once lighted pathways throughout the old resort, were refurbished and hung with baskets of flowers. The resort's famous metal statuary was repaired and placed in various attractive settings to be enjoyed by new generations of visitors. The Coliseum, which now housed a mammoth arcade on the main floor, was given a $100,000 facelift, and the Breakers Hotel was placed on the National Register of Historic Places in 1982. Even the resort's ancient two-wheel fire carts were reconditioned and used to water floral arrangements. Management's blending of much of the old resort with all the spectacular new facilities created a dual atmosphere at Cedar Point that's not found in most other superparks . . . an authentic, harmonious merging of old and new

. . . of yesterday's traditional resort and tomorrow's modern amusement park.

Unfortunately, it was impossible to preserve any of Cedar Point's steamship heritage; however, a group of dedicated Sanduskians were successful in returning the steamer *G. A. Boeckling* to Sandusky after an absence of thirty years. Taken out of service in 1952, the *Boeckling* had been towed to Sturgeon Bay, Wisconsin, where she was used as a floating warehouse for a shipbuilding company. Although she remained structurally sound, her wheelhouses, smokestack and massive engine had been removed. Internally, much of her character remained unchanged. The woodwork of her salon and her main staircase were intact, an ice water sign near a drinking fountain was still legible, and below deck, a razor was found in the crew's quarters exactly where it had been left three decades earlier. In 1980, a non-profit organization, the Friends of the *Boeckling*, was formed, funds were raised, and in 1982, the ship returned to Sandusky. A multi-million dollar restoration effort was begun, with the ultimate goal being that the *Boeckling* could someday be returned to her original operating condition.

By 1975, Cedar Point, Inc. was able to report to shareholders that for thirteen consecutive years the operation's earnings had exceeded those of the previous year. From earnings of $2,500,000 in 1971, the company's annual profits had reached over $10,000,000 in 1982. Attendance at the park set a new record of 2,600,000 in 1975, and exceeded 3,000,000 only three seasons later. Cedar Point, through excellent management and precise planning, had indeed become big business.

Entertaining 3,000,000 guests in a season of just over 100 days requires a highly trained, well-oiled organization. By the late 1970s, Cedar Point was employing as many as 4,300 people in jobs that were mostly seasonal, including ride operators, parking lot attendants, admissions clerks, hotel maids, bellboys, waitresses, cooks, lifeguards, boat operators, sketch artists, entertainers and more. Simply catering to the basic needs of an average of 30,000 guests per day is a logistical challenge, to say the least. The volume of food consumed on the peninsula in just one day could be measured by the ton . . . the drinks, by the thousands of gallons. An entire warehouse was built just to store game prizes and gift shop merchandise. Cedar Point is known to be among the cleanest and best-maintained parks in the world . . . but keeping it that way requires a force of eighty-five college girls who patrol the midway picking up litter. And, the sparkling clean restrooms at Cedar Point can use up to 7,000 rolls of paper hand towels in a single season. With volume such as this, it is truly a testament to Cedar Point's modern management systems and procedures that every guest is treated courteously and

entertained royally, even on the most crowded days.

Now that Cedar Point was once more a bona fide success, management's thoughts turned to expanding, with a new park to be built somewhere in the Midwest and operated on the same principles that had made Cedar Point a dynamic entertainment complex. By the early 1970s, operators of other superparks—Disney, Six Flags and Marriott—were all becoming multi-park owners. The idea of making Cedar Point, Inc. a multi-faceted company was a logical business decision and, accordingly, the directors began scouting locations for their second park.

In June of 1974, Cedar Point's officers announced plans to spend $15,000,000 on a historically themed park to be built fifty miles northwest of Toledo, at Ostend, Michigan. A 1976 opening was projected, but a number of difficulties resulted in a termination of the plan. Instead, they began considering some land near Battle Creek, Michigan. After evaluating more than fifty potential Michigan sites, Cedar Point, Inc. entered into a conditional sales agreement with the City of Battle Creek for the acquisition of 760 acres of land. Cedar Point's projected investment, including $2,000,000 for the land, was expected to be more than $25,000,000; and by the time the park was scheduled to open in 1978, it would feature twenty-six rides and employ a seasonal staff of 1,200. Once again, however, the parties involved could not finalize the details, and for the second time Cedar Point's officers cancelled the project.

Finally, in 1978, plans for a second park materialized. Instead of acquiring vacant land and creating an entirely new facility, however, the company elected to purchase Valleyfair, an already successful turn of the century theme park which had opened in the Minneapolis-St. Paul area in 1976. During the most recent season, Valleyfair had attracted 800,000 visitors and reported gross revenues of $9,000,000. After agreeing upon a purchase price of $15,000,000, Cedar Point appointed a new manager, moved several rides from the Sandusky operation and began operating Valleyfair along the same lines that had made Cedar Point a financial success.

The prosperity that Cedar Point began to enjoy during the 1960s spawned a natural business interest in expansion. But as a publicly held corporation, Cedar Point's glowing annual reports also attracted the attention of other companies that considered the Sandusky park a prime target for acquisition. This acquisition might occur as a merger or a friendly stock purchase, but in an age of aggressive corporate "raiding," it might also come in the form of an unfriendly takeover attempt.

The first hint that Cedar Point might be sold came in May of 1972, when August Busch, Jr. visited Sandusky and met with Emile Legros. Busch's wealthy brewing corporation, Anheuser-Busch, Inc., already operated Busch Gardens, and the acquisition of a midwestern park seemed logical. However, Legros denied all rumors and insisted that Busch had travelled to Sandusky merely to exchange ideas about the amusement park industry and to view the park's new Giant Wheel. Whatever Busch's intentions may have been, Anheuser-Busch made no move to acquire Cedar Point, but six months later an official offer did come from Cincinnati's Taft Broadcasting Company. Experienced in the park business, Taft had been the owner of Cincinnati's beloved Coney Island before closing that old riverside park and constructing the sprawling King's Island facility north of Cincinnati in 1972. According to the proposal, Taft would exchange 1,240,000 shares of Taft stock, worth $67,000,000, for all of the outstanding stock of Cedar Point, Inc. Since Roose and Legros were the principal stockholders, they would exchange their control of Cedar Point for seven-and-one-half percent of Taft Broadcasting. Negotiations continued for a period of time, but when Cedar Point's next annual report was issued, the officers noted that ". . . due to subsequent generally depressed and unstable stock market conditions, the management of both companies concluded that the planned merger should be terminated." But since Cedar Point's revenues reached $25,000,000 in 1972, the shareholders had little reason to lament the termination of the Taft proposal. In 1974, another friendly acquisition proposal was made by the Marriott Corporation, an emerging giant in the amusement park industry. Marriott offered to exchange 1.25 shares of its stock for each share of Cedar Point, Inc., but this $60,000,000 deal also failed when both parties considered the economy and the stock market conditions to be uninviting.

These mergers and sales, since they were approved by the directors, were friendly in nature and were of potential benefit to the shareholders. But late in 1979, an unfriendly takeover attempt surfaced. Earlier, MCA Recreation Enterprises of California had offered a merger proposal that had been rejected by Cedar Point's directors. Now, MCA issued an offer to purchase up to 370,000 shares of Cedar Point stock at thirty-one dollars a share. Since MCA already owned almost 307,000 shares of Cedar Point stock, this offer was properly viewed as a takeover attempt. Fortunately for Cedar Point, its stock was soon trading at thirty-six dollars a share, eliminating any interest in a thirty-one dollar offer.

MCA's attempt to gain control of Cedar Point was unsuccessful, but it made the directors and shareholders painfully aware of the fact that Cedar Point, like any publicly held corporation, was susceptible to an unfriendly takeover. The threat of such takeovers was eliminated when the directors authorized the dissolution of Cedar Point, Inc. and the formation of a new privately owned corporation. The complex task of altering Cedar Point's ownership began in August of 1980, when a British firm, S. Pearson and Son, Ltd., purchased ten percent of the outstanding stock in Cedar Point, Inc. Pearson, the owner of a large portion of England's famed Madame Tussaud's Wax Museum, then offered to buy 519,289 additional shares of stock at $34.95 per share. The directors endorsed Pearson's offer, and by early 1983, an investor group made up of Pearson, Lazard Freres & Company and Robert L. Munger, Jr. bought the remaining outstanding shares of stock for $94,000,000 (at this time, the total value of all stock in Cedar Point, Inc. was about $144,000,000). Despite the objections of some shareholders and the issuance of a temporary restraining order, the sale became final in February of 1983. A new company, Cedar Fair Limited Partnership, was formed and Munger, who had guided the company to profits of $10,400,000 in 1982, became chief executive officer. Free from the fear of hostile takeover attempts, Cedar Point was now prepared to move toward the 1990s and a new era of expansion as one of America's leading recreational centers.

White Water Landing is just one of Cedar Point's collection of great water rides.

Cedar Point

During a single season, the Cedar Point & Lake Erie Railroad carried 2,473,575 passengers.

Cedar Point

By the 1980s, all new Western Cruise boats sailed the lagoons.

Cedar Point

The Antique Cadillac cars, originally installed during the early 1960s, were so popular that a second such ride was built in Frontier Town.

Cedar Point

Live stage shows, staffed by talented college students, were a Cedar Point trademark by the 1970s.

Cedar Point

The Giant Wheel, added in 1972, towers 168 feet above the midway and affords a view of the entire peninsula.

Cedar Point

A quiet and tree-shaded section of the Frontier Trail

Cedar Point

The Frontier Trail's authentic grist mill was moved, stone by stone, from South Carolina.

Cedar Point

The Cedar Creek Mine Ride glides over the waters of the lagoons near Frontier Town.

Cedar Point

Bordering Frontier Town, the Gemini roller coaster created a sensation when it opened in 1978.

Cedar Point

When it was built, the gigantic Gemini was the tallest roller coaster in the world.

Cedar Point

The crowded marina . . . among the largest and finest on the Great Lakes.

Cedar Point

Originally built for Cleveland's Euclid Beach Park in the 1920s, Cedar Downs is among Cedar Point's most unique rides.

Cedar Point

Fully restored, the Coliseum houses a massive arcade on the main floor and maintains the classic 1939 ballroom on the second floor.

Cedar Point

The magnificent floral displays as seen from a car of the Sky Ride.

Cedar Point

One of the park's finest floral creations celebrates Cedar Point's carousel heritage.

A section of Cedar Point with Sandusky Bay and Sandusky in the background.

**Robert L. Munger, Jr.,
who led Cedar Point into
its greatest decades.**

Cedar Point

In 1976, the Corkscrew became one of Cedar Point's most exciting rides.

Cedar Point

Well-trained dolphins and seals love to show off for Cedar Point guests at Oceana.

Cedar Point

The Oceana stadium (left) and Sealand (right).

Cedar Point

Berenstain Bear Country opened in 1985 on the site of the San Francisco Earthquake ride.

Cedar Point

Some of the charming in-
habitants of Bear Country.

Cedar Point

The Cedar Point Cinema houses one of the largest motion picture screens in the world.

Cedar Point

High above the tip of the park's peninsula, the boats of White Water Landing drift toward a watery plunge.

Cedar Point

The forty-five foot plunge on White Water Landing.

Cedar Point

In 1983, the breathtaking Demon Drop was built near the park's admission gates.

Cedar Point

Avalanche Run is an ultra-modern version of the Flying Turns coaster of the 1920s and 1930s.

Cedar Point

Simulating river rafting, Thunder Canyon provides the wetest ride at Cedar Point.

Cedar Point

Penguins enjoy the cold and snow of their habitat at Oceana.

Cedar Point

Jungle Larry and Safari Jane during the 1982 season.

Nancy Jane Tetzlaff-Berens

Berenstain Bear Country provides both entertainment and educational activities for Cedar Point's youngest visitors.

Cedar Point

The midway and Jungle Larry's African Safari as seen from a seat on the Corkscrew.

Chapter Eleven

America's Roller Coast

The untimely death of Robert Munger in November of 1987 signaled the end of one era and the beginning of another at Cedar Point. Associated with Cedar Point since the early 1960s, Munger had been involved in a major portion of the park's development. As president of Cedar Point, Inc., and Cedar Fair L. P., he directed more than $50,000,000 in improvement and expansion programs at the Point. Munger had been a key player in the evolution of Cedar Point, seeing it blossom from a recovering park with limited offerings to one of the nation's most popular amusement facilities. After overseeing the formation of Cedar Fair L. P., Munger watched net revenues swell from $69,359,000 in 1983 to $102,815,000 during the season before his death.

Munger's final contributions to the success of Cedar Point came in the summer of 1987. On April 29, 16,000,000 limited partnership units were made available to investors. Sold at ten dollars per unit, the offering raised more than $147,000,000 for the owners of Cedar Point and proved to be an outstanding investment for the public. By 1993, attendance at all Cedar Fair parks reached 5,511,000, and net revenues climbed to $178,943,000. For investors, this phenomenal performance resulted in a market price that exceeded thirty-five dollars per unit and provided a compound rate of return of more than twenty-four percent.

During Munger's last season at the park, Cedar Point unveiled its seventh roller coaster, the Iron Dragon -- the third suspended coaster to be constructed in the United States. Unlike anything previously seen at the Point, the Iron Dragon has a capacity of 2,000 riders per hour! Each train is comprised of seven four-passenger cars dangling from a half mile of track that loops over the lagoons, through an artificial fog and then plummets to within a few feet of the ground. According to Munger, "…it utilizes the universal image of a dragon, a flying creature that is exciting and mysterious." Justifying its price tag of more than $4,000,000, the Iron Dragon was an immediate success, and by 1993 it ranked fourth in popularity among the park's fifty-six rides. During that season alone, the Iron Dragon thrilled an amazing 1,945,768 riders.

Bob Munger had been aware of his illness for some time; therefore, he was able to work with the board of directors in selecting his successor. They selected Richard Kinzel and their choice could not have been better. A Toledo native who joined the park's food service division in 1972, Kinzel was named director of park operations just three years later. Then, in 1978 he was appointed general manager of Valleyfair. Recognizing Kinzel's executive abilities, park directors elected him vice president of Cedar Point in 1979.

By 1986, Bob Munger's health was steadily declining. No longer able to maintain the hectic pace necessary to direct Cedar Point, he stepped aside. Richard Kinzel became the new president and chief executive officer while Munger took the position of executive chairman of the board. For the first time in 30 years, Cedar Point would be headed by a man not directly associated with the Roose-Legros regime.

Under Richard Kinzel's direction, Cedar Point continued its tradition of installing the industry's largest, most exciting roller coasters. But, Richard Kinzel saw in Cedar Point the potential to be something more than the great amusement park that it already was. His vision for the park included returning it to its former glory as a world-class summer resort, complete with fine dining and luxury accommodations. To this end, he initiated a revival of Cedar Point the Summer Resort. He allocated sizable budgets for new hotel construction and a major renovation of Hotel Breakers. Now Cedar Point could truly say it had something for everyone -- from the intense excitement of the midway to the relaxing luxury of waterfront accommodations.

It was no surprise that Cedar Point became known as the world leader in roller coasters. Since the beginning, the park had always been at the forefront of roller coaster technology. Cedar Point's first roller coaster, The Switchback Railway, was installed in 1892, only eight years after the first such device was erected at Coney Island, New York. By the 1920s, Cedar Point was operating three large coasters in an era when few parks had

The Iron Dragon dives to within a few feet of the lagoons.

Cedar Point

In 1991, when Cedar Point added the Mean Streak, the mammoth ride was the world's tallest and fastest wooden roller coaster.

Cedar Point

more than one. The Cyclone, built in 1929, was unquestionably one of the most exciting coasters in the Midwest for decades. But when it comes to size, speed, sensation, and ride technology, even the Cyclone couldn't compare with the coasters built during the 1980s and 1990s.

At the end of the 1987 season, Cedar Point's management and planning personnel determined that the park's roller coasters had accommodated 11,500,000 riders during that season. They also recognized that the roller coaster was in the midst of a rebirth of popularity throughout the world. Consequently, the growth of Cedar Point during the late 1980s and early 1990s closely paralleled the evolution of modern roller coaster technology.

In 1989, Cedar Point stunned the coaster-riding public with the installation of the Magnum XL-200. The $8,000,000 all-steel monster was the tallest, steepest, and fastest coaster in the world. Its trains climb to the top of an incredible 205-foot lift hill then plunge down a sixty-degree descent at seventy-two miles per hour to a point only eleven feet above the ground. Very nearly as thrilling as the first drop, the ride's second hill towers 157 feet in the air and leads to one of three tunnels situated on the ride. Standing near the coaster's exit to personally hear the comments of the riders, Dick Kinzel heard this gratifying comment: "The greatest roller coaster on earth!" The Magnum XL-200 quickly justified the high cost of its installation. During its first season, the ride thrilled 1,800,000 courageous people. At the same time, Cedar Fair L. P.'s operating revenues set all-time records, exceeding those of 1988 by sixteen percent. It would seem that roller coasters, despite their long history and enormous price tags, are still excellent investments.

The Magnum XL-200 made such a huge impression that any ride introduced in 1990 would necessarily be judged by the Magnum's standards. Instead of designing a new ride based on speed or height, it was decided to convert Avalanche Run into Disaster Transport, a futuristic, themed space transport. To accomplish this, the existing ride was enclosed in a building painted to simulate a battered and worn launching facility. Inside, more than 150 props were installed, including animated devices, robots, lasers, projectors, wind blast machinery, and audio-visual equipment. Upon entering the ride, passengers are informed that they are about to take part in a mission to deliver a cargo to Earth. Along the way, they experience a variety of perilous adventures. Disaster Transport is the first Cedar Point ride to take full advantage of modern visual technology, providing an attraction that appeals more to the senses than to a craving for speed and height. Long lines of riders snaked into Disaster Transport all season, but predictably, the ride failed to generate the incredible excitement that greeted the Magnum XL-200 a season earlier.

Challenged to create a ride to equal or surpass the Magnum XL-200, Cedar Point's planning staff hired noted roller coaster engineer Curtis D. Summers to design the world's largest wooden coaster for the 1991 season. Summers was one of several men responsible for the renaissance of wooden roller coasters. From the 1890s through the 1920s, thousands of wooden coasters were built throughout the world. However, new construction nearly came to a standstill during the 1930s and saw only a limited resurgence in the late 1940s and 1950s. By the 1970s, all-steel roller coasters dominated the market, and few traditional wooden roller coasters of any magnitude were designed. A swing back to classic wooden rides was underway by the 1980s , and Summers, who designed his first coaster in 1967, was one of the stars of the revitalized industry. Prior to designing the new ride for Cedar Point, Summers' greatest contribution to the industry was the Hercules, a 157-foot high coaster built in 1989 at Dorney Park in Allentown, Pennsylvania.

The ride Summers created for Cedar Point, was appropriately named the Mean Streak. An imposing mountain of wood containing 1,700,000 feet of treated Southern yellow pine, the Mean Streak features graceful banked curves, twelve hills and valleys, and a course that crisscrosses the structure nine times. The first hill looms 161 feet above the midway and starts a 5,427-foot course that enables trains to reach speeds of up to sixty-five miles per hour. Although Mean Streak debuted during an economic recession, this superb coaster helped Cedar Point post increased net revenues. As Richard Kinzel stated after the close of the season, "When fighting a recession, it's good to have a 161-foot, 65 mph 'Mean Streak' on your side." With its tremendous speed and high volume capacity, the Mean Streak was able to handle 4,700,000 passengers during its first three seasons.

In 1992, Cedar Point celebrated one hundred years of roller coasters at the resort. Technology had advanced a great deal from the 1892 Switchback Railway, with its maximum height of twenty-five feet and speed of less than ten miles per hour. The Point's new coasters boasted nearly ten times the height and seven times the speed. But, as advanced as roller coaster engineering was by 1991, Cedar Point still sought new frontiers in ride design.

After directing investments toward other additions and improvements in 1992 and 1993, Cedar Point again astounded the coaster-riding public with a new thriller for the 1994 season. Of the incredible Raptor, Richard Kinzel said, "It will set the pace for the next century of roller coasters and will long be remembered for changing the look of Cedar Point." Indeed, the Raptor altered the appearance of the park, for in order to place the new $12,000,000 coaster near the entrance to the midway it

The breathtaking 205-foot first hill of the Magnum XL-200, the tallest and fastest roller coaster in the world. The Gemini roller coaster is in the background.

Cedar Point

was necessary to dismantle the Mill Race, relocate the Calypso, and install the classic Midway Carousel in a new building behind the admission complex. At 137 feet high, the Raptor is an inverted coaster with ski lift-type seats suspended below the track in thirty-two passenger trains. Raptor passengers turn upside down on the outside of its structure six times during the circuit. As the tallest, fastest, and steepest coaster of its kind in the world, Raptor features a "cobra roll," a design element never before included on a roller coaster, During the cobra roll, trains spiral upside down, negotiate a 180-degree roll, and then repeat the spiralling motion as they move out of the cobra roll and head back for the station. The 360-degree barrel rolls, accomplished at up to fifty-seven miles per hour, leave even the most experienced coaster riders weak-kneed and a bit shaky.

The addition of the Raptor brought Cedar Point's coaster total to eleven - - the largest collection in the world. Even Chicago's Riverview Park, once the nation's roller coaster capital, never approached this number of high rides. And, with more than 16,000,000 people enjoying Cedar Point's coasters each summer, the park has certainly earned the nickname, "America's Roller Coast."

Although it may seem that Cedar Point's development in the 1980s and 1990s focused on the construction of record-breaking roller coasters, management was actually very careful to plan a balanced expansion of the park. Like George Boeckling, who expanded the beach and excavated the lagoons, Dick Kinzel is committed to ensuring that the park also caters to those who love the water. Water rides had been installed at Cedar Point in the 1960s and 1970s, but the first major effort to feature water activities at the park came in 1986 with the construction of Thunder Canyon. Simulating white water rafting, Thunder Canyon's twelve-passenger circular rafts float wildly through 1600 feet of raging rapids and under waterfalls, drenching riders with torrents of water. The 900,000 gallons of Lake Erie water filling Thunder Canyon are whipped into a frenzy of rapids by four 200-horsepower pumps. Not surprisingly, Thunder Canyon is especially popular on hot days, for few emerge from the ride without being totally soaked.

Thunder Canyon was an immediate success and proved capable of handling more than one and a half million riders each season. The public's enthusiasm for this ride prompted management to investigate additional water attractions. In 1988, water parks were gaining popularity throughout the country, often being built adjacent to or within amusement parks. Clearly, the time was right for the debut of Cedar Point's Soak City.

A first-class waterpark with outstanding facilities, Soak City was constructed just beyond Hotel Breakers, with Lake Erie as the perfect backdrop, Located on five acres, Soak City boasts more than 4,100 feet of fiberglass slides including three body slides, two inner tube slides, three raft slides, and two speed slides. Ranging in height from twenty-four to sixty-six feet, the speed-slides drop steeply at the same angle as the Gemini roller coaster. The facility requires 210,000 gallons of water, which is filtered and re-circulated every hour. Although an extremely hot 1988 season resulted in a slight decline in park attendance, Soak City helped increase per capita spending by five per cent. Soak City's success inspired the park to expand the attraction in 1990 by adding the Main Stream -- a 1,200-foot artificial river whose slow-moving current carries inner-tube riders along at a leisurely pace. Tadpole Town was also added. The play area is specifically for younger children and features water jets, slides, water curtains, tunnels and a tire swing.

In 1993, Cedar Point amplified their water facilities even further with the construction of Snake River Falls, the most spectacular water flume ever built. Based on the Shoot-the-Chutes ride invented during the 1890s, Snake River Falls takes the old concept to a whole new dimension in height and speed. The ride's twenty-passenger boats are first lifted to the top of a steep, eighty-two foot hill. Then they plunge into a lake below at forty miles per hour. Upon hitting the water, the boats create a 1,600-square-foot tidal wave drenching spectators on an observation bridge located in the ride's "splash zone." Snake River Falls was an instant success with older children and adults. But to make sure that even the park's youngest patrons could enjoy a new water ride, Kiddy Bumper boats were installed in Kiddy Kingdom. According to Richard Kinzel, "With these two rides, we are going to get the entire family wet this summer."

Snake River Falls had the good fortune to be introduced during a warm, dry, pleasant summer. As a result, Cedar Point's attendance soared to new heights, The previous record, set in 1989 with the opening of the Magnum XL-200, was broken by more than 100,000 admissions during Snake River Fall's premier season.

Throughout the 1980s and early 1990s, the development of Cedar Point centered on the construction of large, record-setting rides representing multi-million dollar investments. As Cedar Fair's 1988 annual report stated, "Big rides have always figured prominently in the popularity of our parks. Roller Coasters differentiate the great amusement parks from all the others, providing excitement on a grand scale and diversifying the mix of family activities that appeal to all ages." While big roller coasters dominated the expansion program, park planners were careful to balance the super rides with a wide range of other entertainment activities. A significant example of such diversification is Challenge Park constructed in 1992 between Soak City and Hotel Breakers. Located outside of the park gates on two acres of land, the first

The incredible Raptor negotiates the unique "cobra roll".

Cedar Point

phase of Challenge Park was the Grand Prix raceway. In go-karts designed to look like Grand Prix race cars, drivers race at speeds of up to twenty miles per hour around a 1,500-foot track, across a bridge, and through two tunnels. A season later, Challenge Golf, consisting of two eighteen-hole miniature golf courses, was added. Challenge Park, which includes Soak City, has greatly broadened the variety of activities offered at the Point.

Another example of Cedar Point's diversification is the extensive expansion of Berenstain Bear Country. In 1992, the popular indoor attraction was enlarged to include a sizable outdoor section. The indoor facility was transformed into Berenstain Bear Science Fair, where science and biology exhibits invite youngsters to participate in a fun learning experience. Outside, parents can watch from a special observation gazebo as children explore the Spooky Old Tree, ride the miniature train, and tour the Bear Family Tree House.

Fulfilling its promise to entertain guests of all ages, Cedar Point completely revamped and expanded Kiddieland for the 1993 season. Renamed Kiddy Kingdom, the area's new medieval decor features bright colors, flags, and special lighting. The continued development of rides and themed areas for youngsters is proof of the park's commitment to offer something for every member of the family.

Cedar Point's live entertainment package has few equals in the amusement industry. The park's spectacular stage shows are consistently updated and feature the finest high school and college talent in the nation. From the Broadway tunes at Lusty Lil's Palace to Dixieland hits at the Red Garter Saloon, the entertainment is non-stop and top-notch. The musical bill of fare has been broadened to appeal to every taste from high school bands strolling the midway to jazz, country, rock and roll, Top 40, and music of the 1950s and 1960s. It would be difficult to find a more well-balanced offering of live musical entertainment and beautifully staged shows. In fact, for many, a visit to Cedar Point is not complete until they have enjoyed all of the park's live entertainment shows.

Although Frontier Trail is one of the park's older attractions, it has never shown its age or lost its charm. Because Frontier Trail connects the older main midway with the newer section at the rip of the peninsula, it is one of the Point's major pedestrian thoroughfares. Always beautifully maintained, Frontier Trail provides a cool, tree-shaded respite from the bustling excitement of the main midway. Since 1989, the trail's grist mill has presented authentic flour milling exhibitions while other buildings scattered along the trail feature traditional candlemaking, glassblowing, blacksmithing, and pottery production.

First introduced in the mid-70s, Cedar Point's gigantic Cinema is still a popular draw. Equipped with six-track stereo and two "surround" channels, the Cinema virtually draws spectators into the film's action. From a tour of Ontario's wilderness to a trip through outer space, the Cedar Point Cinema uses the latest technology in sight and sound to make the viewer feel like he or she is at the center of the action. In 1992, the Cedar Point Cinema became the first amusement park theatre to show the 1990 summer tour of the Rolling Stones.

By 1994 Jungle Larry's African Safari had been in continuous operation longer than any other show at Cedar Point. After Jungle Larry's death, David Tetzlaff followed in the footsteps of his famous father by introducing park visitors to new acts and unusual animals. In 1989 a pack of seven wolves was installed in a new training area, and Tetzlaff introduced his unique wolf act. A year later, the African Safari exhibited a rare white tiger cub and a Golden Tabby Bengal tiger, one of only thirteen in the world. Tetzlaff continued to produce amazing tiger acts, and his leopard act featuring twelve cats, was the largest of its kind in the United States. Like Jungle Larry before him, David Tetzlaff dedicated much of his time and effort to educating the public about animals and fostering a better understanding of their habits and habitats. He created the Safari Canyon Wildlife Lectures, during which trainers bring wild animals within an arm's reach of the park's visitors.

David Tetzlaff and his mother, Nancy "Safari Jane" Tetzlaff-Berens, also own Caribbean Gardens, a successful animal park in Naples, Florida. As the Florida park grew, it became increasingly difficult to operate both facilities. Logistics were especially difficult -- shipping animals and personnel north to Cedar Point every spring and back again to Florida in the fall became more of a challenge each year. Reluctantly, the decision was made to concentrate all efforts on the Caribbean Gardens, and in August of 1994, it was announced that Jungle Larry's African Safari was completing its last season at the Point. After thirty seasons at Cedar Point in addition to earlier runs at Huron Kiddieland, Crystal Beach Park, Puritas Springs Park, and Chippewa Lake Park, Jungle Larry's famous exotic wildlife exhibits would cease to be an important part of Ohio's amusement park scene.

Another sad event was the destruction of the steamer *G. A. Boeckling* on June 21, 1989. While funds were being raised for the restoration of the vessel, she was sent to a Toledo shipyard for some necessary work. A suspicious fire broke out during the night, reducing the ship to nothing more than a floating wreck. With all woodwork destroyed the decks buckled, and the hull damaged, the Friends of the *Boeckling* reluctantly admitted that the old steamer was beyond repair. The dream to return the famous Cedar Point ferry to service on Sandusky Bay had gone up in smoke.

On opening day of the 1993 season, Snake River Falls creates a wall of water that is about to engulf spectators standing on the bridge.

Cedar Point

Soak City, which is situated on the shore of Lake Erie, is one of the best waterparks in the nation.   Cedar Point

Meanwhile, attendance at Cedar Point continued to increase each year. In terms of attendance, the four Disney parks are rated as the largest parks in America, with a combined annual total of more than 41,000,000 people. Cedar Point ranks number nine in attendance. It must be noted, however, that parks ranking one through eight in attendance are located in California and Florida, which gives them the distinct advantage of a year-long season. From 970,000 people in 1959, Cedar Point's annual attendance had climbed to 3,068,000 by 1987. According to an industry trade magazine, the number of visitors reached 3,600,000 in 1993. During that season, Cedar Point's fifty-six rides hosted an incredible 43,918,043 thrill-seekers! What were the most popular rides of 1993? Here's a list of the top ten;

Gemini	3,336,306
C. P. & L. E. Railroad	2,473,575
Magnum XL-200	2,201,951
Iron Dragon	1,945,768
Corkscrew	1,862,146
Sky Ride	1,719,468
Cedar Creek Mine Ride	1,680,592
Mean Streak	1,643,445
Thunder Canyon	1,576,525
Blue Streak	1,485,205

Obviously, multi-million dollar thrill rides are the major attraction at Cedar Point, but when not riding, park patrons spend much of their time enjoying the delicious foods and snacks that are offered along the midway and throughout the park. Cedar Point's excellent food service has grown to keep pace with attendance. Today, hungry visitors can select their snacks and treats from among more than fifty food stands, carts, and restaurants -- all operated by a seasonal staff that exceeds 1,500 employees. Perennial midway favorites include Cedar Point's famous french fries (rated among the top ten in the country by amusement park devotees), saltwater taffy, soft pretzels, hot caramel apples topped with peanuts, and frozen yogurt dipped in fudge and covered with walnuts. In fact, the list of dining choices at the Point is almost endless, and the volume of food and drink consumed each season is staggering. In 1993, visitors consumed 300,000 pounds of hamburger patties, 75 tons of cheese, 153,800 pounds of hot dogs, 65,300 pounds of french fries, and 16,800 gallons of hand-scooped ice cream. Then washed it all down with more than 611,600 gallons of Pepsi Cola products.

Even the animals at Cedar Point eat well! In 1993, Oceana's dolphins consumed 29,000 pounds of food, the two sea lions ate another 8,000 pounds, and the baby animals at the Petting Farm on Frontier Trail downed an amazing 58,000 bottles of milk.

Cedar Point's live shows have been a popular part of the park for more than thirty years.

Cedar Point

Richard Kinzel, the driving force behind the Cedar Point of the 1990's.

Cedar Point

Don Miears, Cedar Point's general manager and executive vice-president.

Cedar Point

The popular Grand Prix raceway in Challenge Park.

Cedar Point

While catching a fast bite between rides is the goal of most park visitors, many opt for a more leisurely meal in one of the park's many sit-down restaurants. The Bay Harbor Inn, Dominics, Macaroni's, the Silver Dollar Cafe, the Red Garter Saloon, the Last Chance Saloon, the Chuck Wagon Inn, and the Marina Steak House offer everything from pizza and sandwiches to perfectly prepared steaks and lobster dinners. The list of fine restaurants was expanded in 1991 with the opening of the Breakwater Cafe at the very tip of Cedar Point. Intended to serve hotel guests and park visitors, Breakwater Cafe's contemporary design offers diners a breathtaking view of the entrance to Sandusky Bay complete with passing ships, pleasure boats, and those spectacular sunsets.

Two years after the opening of the Breakwater Cafe, the Marina Steak House on the bay pier was redecorated to debut as The Boathouse. A specialty of The Boathouse is barbecued ribs made with an exclusive recipe developed by Ribs King of Cincinnati. Cedar Point is the only location outside of Cincinnati to feature the barbecue recipe favored by former President Gerald Ford, entertainer Bob Hope, and sport figures Johnny Bench and Pete Rose.

The need for additional restaurants at Cedar Point was due in part to an increase in the resort's overnight accommodations. The closing of the old Hotel Cedars, the razing of one of the sections of the Hotel Breakers, and the conversion of some of the older sections of the Breakers to employee housing gradually reduced the number of guest rooms at the Point. Although the rooms in the Breakers were remodeled during the 1960s, no new rooms had been added. Meanwhile, Cedar Point was becoming one of the region's most popular destinations. As families travelled to the Point from other states and even from other countries, the facilities at Hotel Breakers were stretched to the limit. Every July and August the hotel was booked to capacity and many guests who wanted to stay overnight on the peninsula were forced to find rooms in the Sandusky area.

Obviously, it was time to build new accommodations. The first step toward that goal was the construction of the $4,000,000, ninety-six unit Sandcastle Suites Hotel built in 1990. The first new hotel at Cedar Point since 1915, Sandcastle Suites is located west of the Hotel Breakers near the tip of the peninsula where it offers a peaceful respite from the noise and activity of the park's midway. In addition to its own beautiful beach, the hotel features an outdoor swimming pool, a gift shop, and tennis courts.

The new Sandcastle Suites proved so popular that in 1992, two more wings were added for a grand total of 187 suites. Once again patios or balconies were constructed for new suites that also feature two queen-sized beds, a sleeper sofa and refrigerator. For the ultimate in total relaxation the hotel's three Grand Vista Suites are

outfitted with whirlpools and large decks or patios facing Lake Erie.

Amid all the new construction, the venerable Hotel Breakers was enjoying a major renovation of its own. In 1991, an ice cream parlor was installed just off the lobby which was undergoing a total facelift! The entire lobby, including its original molded tin ceiling, was carefully painted, new wallpaper was hung and carpeting was laid, and even the hotel's famous round couches were restored and reupholstered. A beautiful swimming pool appeared in front of the Surf Lounge, poolside hotel rooms were totally redecorated and refurnished, and in 1992, both the Breakers and Sandcastle Suites could boast of new whirlpool spas. By the early 1990s, Cedar Point was once again the popular summer resort it had been from 1905 to the late 1920s.

Cedar Point was now a unique blending of the world's greatest amusement park, a major vacation destination, and a summer resort that rivaled many of the famous oceanside retreats. By 1993, the total combined revenues of all of the Cedar Fair operations had reached $178,943,000. Even so, Cedar Point management never lost sight of the park's obligation to its community. Cedar Point's charitable contributions include generous donations to pediatric facilities and children's causes throughout the Sandusky area. In 1992, Cedar Point's aluminum can recycling effort raised funds for the Burned Children's Program of Northwest Ohio. Demonstrating its concern for the environment, the park has substituted gasohol for gasoline in all of its Turnpike cars, Antique cars, Paddlewheel Excursion boats, Grand Prix go-karts, courtesy cars, and even lawn mowers. Moreover, wherever possible, recycled paper is used. The park's decision to use Envision tissue products, made from 100 percent recycled materials, had a major environmental impact. In 1993 alone, it was estimated that Cedar Point had conserved 471,600 gallons of water, 276,200 kilowatts of electricity, 1,100 trees, and 202 cubic yards of landfill space.

While Cedar Point grew continuously throughout the 1980s and into the 1990s, Cedar Fair's other park, Valleyfair, also prospered, usually entertaining about 1,000,000 visitors per summer. The success of these parks encouraged Richard Kinzel and the directors of Cedar Fair to search for another acquisition. This search resulted in the purchase of Dorney Park and the adjacent Wildwater Kingdom in Allentown, Pennsylvania. Purchased in 1992 at a cost of approximately $48,000,000, Dorney Park was one of the great names in American amusement park history. Solomon Dorney first opened his "Fish Weir & Summer Resort" in 1860. In 1884 the little resort became Dorney Park and gradually grew into a well-known amusement park. During the 1980s, Dorney underwent a major expansion program that included the construction of a multi-million dollar waterpark, Wildwater Kingdom. This was followed in 1989 by the construction of Hercules, at that time the world's tallest wooden coaster.

The acquisition of Dorney Park had an immediate positive effect on Cedar Point's parent organization. Dorney's market area combined with those of Cedar Point and Valleyfair totalled 65,000,000 potential park visitors. During its first season under Cedar Fair management, Dorney Park and Wildwater Kingdom accounted for 600,000 of the 4,860,000 people who visited the Cedar Fair parks.

During 1995 Cedar Point marks its 125th anniversary as a summer resort and amusement facility. A handful of other parks have reached this milestone, but only Cedar Point can boast that at 125 years of age, it's just reaching its peak! New York's Coney Island survives, but just barely and only as a shadow of its former self. Atlantic City also survives, but only steps away from the glamour of the casinos the once-great boardwalk has become a shoddy avenue littered with the remains of amusement piers and shops. Only resorts like New Jersey's Ocean City and Cape May can claim to have maintained their positions as popular summer resorts.

A month before the close of the 1994 season, Cedar Point's public relations staff was announcing plans for the 125th season. In celebration, $17,000,000 has been slated for park improvements and new construction. While this represents the largest expenditure in the history of Cedar Point, it's but a small portion of the $93,000,000 that has been spent on capital improvements since 1986.

Topping the list of improvements for 1995 is the new $10,000,000 Breakers East wing of the Hotel Breakers. Responding to the great demand for the newly renovated rooms at the Breakers, management considered a variety of ways for improving and expanding the hotel. Determining that renovation of the old wings of the hotel was impractical, it was decided that the wooden structures would be demolished and replaced with a new wing combining modern comfort with turn-of-the-century charm. Designed to blend with the Breakers' original architecture, the Breakers East includes 102 rooms, 95 lakeview suites, and 8 tower suites. Located on five acres, the new hotel complex also features an outdoor swimming pool, spa, and conference and meeting center. The opening of Breakers East brings the total number of guest rooms at the Breakers to 496, while the total number of hotel rooms at Cedar Point approaches 700.

Additional plans for 1995 call for yet another expansion of Soak City. According to Don Miears, executive vice president and general manager of Cedar Point, "The top two things our guests request over and over again are roller coasters and water rides." The latest Soak City expansion more than doubles the size of the waterpark which is dominated by a high-action slide with large circular rafts seating six passengers. The rafts float in a thirteen-foot wide flume designed with steeply-banked sides that enable the rafts to crest at an angle of nearly ninety degrees. Another Soak City attraction is a 1300-foot inner tube stream that offers riders the choice of two courses: the first is a gentle, slow moving stream; the other includes wave and bubble generators, geysers, and cascading waterfalls. Two activity pools with slides and chutes, and a smaller version of the inner tube river has been added for younger guests.

In 1899, George Boeckling noted, "One can scarcely picture a more delightful spot wherein to while the sultry days of summer." Seven years later, his advertising manager wrote, "When nature modeled Cedar Point she fashioned the perfect design and provided every natural advantage for a tourist metropolis of illimitable possibilities. Man here found a flawless foundation on which to build, so that the remarkable facts of a later date have been only in keeping with the early history of this grand spot." Yet the "remarkable facts" of 1906, although spectacular for the time, pale in comparison to the Cedar Point of 1995. Late in his life, George Boeckling declared that Cedar Point was still in its infancy. As grand as the Cedar Point of the 1920s was, Boeckling envisioned an even greater Cedar Point for future generations to enjoy. However, it's probably safe to say that the Cedar Point of 1995 far exceeds even the wildest of Boeckling's dreams!

Cedar Point's 125th season is historically significant because very few summer resorts and amusement parks have survived long enough to reflect the rise, decline, and rebirth of the American public amusement facility. Cedar Point emerged at a time when memories of the Civil War were still fresh and there was plenty of frontier left to settle. The resort shared its infancy with other popular amusements, including music halls, vaudeville, theaters, dance halls, circuses, the concert band, the amusement park, the world's fair, and even the moving picture theater. In fact, many of these entertainments would become integral parts of the Cedar Point entertainment complex. When amusement parks became America's favorite summertime diversion, Cedar Point spawned its own amusement circle. Later, like so many resorts, the Point suffered at the hands of the Prohibitionists. Following the First World War, when all of the traditional public amusements began to fade rapidly, Cedar Point began a slow decline that lasted for more than twenty years. The 1920s provided the owners of the park with an excellent income, but the prosperity of the decade was uneven and unpredictable. Boeckling was one of many who recognized that the economy was fragile and unbalanced. As a result, he made few major improvements after 1925.

Sandcastle Suites Hotel offers a private beach, a swimming pool complex, and a magnificent view of Lake Erie.

Cedar Point

Recent improvements at Hotel Breakers have included the installation of a swimming pool and the complete renovation of the rooms facing the pool area.

Cedar Point

Breakers East, developed for the 125th Anniversary season, is designed to perfectly compliment the original 1905 architecture of Hotel Breakers.

Cedar Point

The depression of the 1930s hastened the decline of amusement parks and summer resorts that had begun during the previous decade. Throughout the summer resort industry, the wave of energy that had been in evidence since at least the 1890s finally ebbed. In Atlantic City, the last of the great hotels was constructed in the 1930's, and at Coney Island, the last of the major roller coasters rose during the late 1920s. Although Coney's Steeplechase Park would struggle on until 1964, Luna Park barely survived until it was razed by fire after the Second World War. Across the country amusement parks closed their gates, summer resorts disappeared, and great summer hotels were demolished. In northern Ohio and southeastern Michigan, most of Cedar Point's longtime competitors vanished between the 1930s and 1960s. Among those that could no longer tolerate declining attendance and losing seasons were Detroit's Eastwood Park, Toledo's Walbridge Park, Genoa's Forest Park, Vermilion's Crystal Beach Park, and in Cleveland, Puritas Springs Park and Euclid Beach Park. All had once competed with Cedar Point for the entertainment dollar.

Obviously, the fact that Cedar Point lost most of its competition certainly contributed to the resort's chances for survival. However, in the late 1940s and again in 1956, Cedar Point was desperately near the point of extinction.

Were it not for the dedication of Dan Schneider and the business acumen of George Roose, the chances of Cedar Point reaching its 125th anniversary would have been slim indeed. Schneider, with more faith than money, began to slowly revive the failing resort in the

early 1950s. Roose, blessed with extensive resources and a sound business plan, took over where Schneider left off and implemented a growth plan in the mid-50s that is still obvious in 1995. Fortunately, men like Robert Munger and Richard Kinzel not only understood Roose's plans but improved upon them, expanding them to a point not even imaginable in the 1960s and '70s.

In a way, Schneider, Roose, Legros, Munger, and Kinzel could be considered descendants of the astute George A. Boeckling. Like him, they saw in Cedar Point the potential for something more than a run-of-the-mill amusement park. They envisioned a truly great family entertainment facility. An amusement park, yes…but more than that, a place of beautiful white sandy beaches and luxury hotels and first-class restaurants. A true summer resort in every sense of the word…with something for people of all ages. No doubt Boeckling, who in the 1920s insisted that Cedar Point's greatest years were still in the future, would be very proud of his beautiful peninsula.

Leaving

CEDAR POINT

AFTER A

· BIG · DAY ·

COMING
HOME
BROKE

Leaving Cedar Point. Tired but happy . . . and already looking forward to next year!

Tim Dagg Collection

Index

About the authors:

A graduate of Baldwin-Wallace College, David Francis has written more than two dozen magazine and journal articles and has been a contributor to *The Encyclopedia of Southern History*. Diane Francis majored in English at the University of Akron before pursuing a career as an advertising copywriter in Akron and New York.

The Francis' collaboration began in the mid-1980s when they began to research the first edition of *Cedar Point: The Queen Of American Watering Places*. Since the publication of their first book, they have co-authored three additional works and are currently working on a fourth.

Building on more than 20 years' experience in the advertising business, the Francis' founded their own advertising agency in Wadsworth, Ohio, in 1990. Married since 1981, Dave and Diane share their home with several dogs and cats.

ERRATA

Page	For	Read
10, line 8	*Ceder Point*	*Cedar Point*
98, line 12	Cold Cascades	Old Cascades
98, line 32	Edan Musee	Eden Musee
back cover, line 19	*Ceder Point*	*Cedar Point*
back cover, line 22	*Foreward*	*Foreword*
96	delete 5 from Racer Roller Coaster (4)	

"America's Roller Coast", September 1, 1993. Photo by Dan Feicht.
Cedar Point